Becoming Oneness

the Art of Transformation

Nalini MacNab

Becoming Oneness: The Art of Transformation

Copyright © 2020 by Nalini MacNab

All rights reserved. This book or parts thereof may not be reproduced in any form, stored in any retrieval system, or transmitted in any form by any means–electronic, mechanical, photocopy, recording, or otherwise–without prior written permission of the publisher

Dedication

If you grew up sensitive, differently attuned to nature than most, aware of your wings but unable to find them;
If you know, in each cell of your body what is possible;
If your understanding of life is based in reverence for the love that created us;
This is for you.

To the Light that illuminates us all, this is for YOU.

Table of Contents

Why This Book?.. 1
Foreword... 3
Introduction 8
Becoming Fluid ~... 11
    What does it mean to become flow? 11
    How is an Enlightened Embodiment like Becoming a Butterfly? 12
    The Orb of Light 14
    Feeding the Sense of Self 16
    Why is Creativity a Necessity? 18
The Nature of Our Agreements 19
    What is an Agreement? 22
    Starting with the Personality 23
    What About Lifetime Agreements? 26
Dumping Unnecessary Data.. 36
    The big picture is bigger than what we believe............... 36
    How do we let go into HER big picture? 38
Sacred Feminine Enlightenment... 40
    Enter Emily 42
    Emily's Exit 42
The Heartspace 44
    Initiation.. 44
    The Heartspace 46

How to Visualize the HeartSpace 47
Understanding the Heartspace 50
The Chrysalis 59
The Newly-Awakening 60
The Reality Construct 65
The Setup for Becoming~ Preparing to Spin a Chrysalis 75
Meditation 76
What is Meditation and Why Does it Matter? 76
What meditation techniques work best for dissolution into Her Oneness? 77
Minding the Mind ~ Mindfulness 85
What's wrong with the way we think? 87
Thought Patterns 89
Belief Systems 90
Habits of Behavior 91
Movement 95
Transformation 99
Shifting From the Heart 101
Lifting the Veils of Separation 101
Why Listen, and How? 102
The Difference Between Hearing and Listening 104
Her Spherical Morphing Wave 111
Daily Practice 113
Beginning the Day 113
Ending the Day 114
Archetypal Allegiances 115

How to Release Archetypal Allegiance 120
Shifting Genetic Patterns ~ Using epigenetics to your advantage 130
    Inception 131
    Conception 132
    Imprints and Implants 134
    Bloodlines 137
Symptom Causing Patterns 140
Conception Point Release Meditation 155
Shifting Core Agendas 160
What Will You Make REAL? 165
Beyond the Butterfly 171
Conclusion 173
About the Author 174
Bibliography 176

Why This Book?

The information in this book belongs to the Sacred Feminine, the Great Mother. I have scribed and taught it for decades – about thirty if we're counting. Before that, I lived it, as have you, each in our own way. For me, it was conscious, for you it might not have been, or perhaps partly so.

When I was a child, The Great Mother stalked me in earnest. I learned Her love in our tiny back garden, among the trees and flowers. When my family moved from a flat in the city to a house in the country, I thought I had gone to heaven. {Ssh! Don't tell anyone... it might be taken away.} I spent much of my growing years immersed in the world of nature. I learned to be quiet and still, to let the woods speak to me instead of the other way 'round. I loved all things four-legged, especially horses.

When the family moved again, I did not move with them. Things had changed for me. Though I had no idea at the time, I was about to be taken on a Great Adventure.

It wasn't time to put away *childlike* things, but to end *childish* points of view and step into what is possible.

What is *your* Great Adventure? What if it lies in the realms of paying attention? Of allowing yourself to become fully conscious of life, instead of letting your subconscious dictate your life experiences? What if, in becoming a conscious participant in Oneness, your experience of living moved into one of magic, miracles, and divine manifestation?

It is Her wish, and my hope, that you will find in this book ways to keep pace with a multiverse in transition, understanding of how your lifetime has been directed until now, and a growing sense of your birthright within Divine embrace.

We are all part of Her Oneness, fractals within Her waves.

May Her Art of Transformation be a blessing to you as it has been to me.

Foreword

This book is both story and self-help for those caterpillars who want(ed) to become a butterfly more than anything. We began our transformation under the influence of existing, traditional systems of spirituality, only to find their sands shifting out from under our feet. Joy! Confusion. What is the way? Is there a way? Why do the traditional paths no longer seem to work in the old way?

The Great Mother, Creatrix of all things that are, have been, and will be, *is* all ways that have ever been and will ever be. She opens new frequencies, new realms, untrodden paths for us, right under our feet.

This is a testimony to Her Presence, the doorway through Her Heart, and how to practice this becoming.

***

Emily wanted Enlightenment more than anything once she learned this term for becoming one with the divine. She read the books of the book religions, discovering they were not what she sought. She studied Eastern and Western mysticism. Closer, but her heart remained unsatisfied.

The Goddess traditions she saved for a rainy day, due to a complicated relationship with her birth mother. Emily learned to love her mother dearly, but from a safe distance.

She felt a part of nature, as well as the clear light, the golden light, the blue-white light she remembered as home. She remembered the magic. And yet, that safe distance remained.

The Great Mother, beseeched ten thousand times by as many different names, finally shook Emily by the scruff and enfolded her in loving arms, letting her know she had answered *every time*, ten thousand times before.

Surrendering into her Creatrix, Emily's safe distance began to melt. She learned appropriate boundaries and how to let them serve her. She learned her shields and allies. And, leaving all traditions behind as the gifts they had been, she lightened her cocoon and broke free of her self-woven chrysalis. Her open heart spread its wings, ready to fly.

Emily's first request to her primary teacher was, "Teach me to fly like that!" And, always listening, always cherishing, *the Great Mother did*.

Let's Talk Enlightenment

Before we go any further, let's review the term 'Enlightenment'. I have heard many very aware individuals declare they no longer have an interest in the Enlightenment process. Fair enough. The old, hierarchical ways will not support our evolution in most of Her new realities.

For those who assert, "I want a reality where the old ways work!" there will be bandwidths of that available. For Gaia, though, the old realities are no longer what she chooses to support. These will fade and disappear.

Why use the term Enlightenment at all? For those who yearn after the light, it grabs attention. Enlightenment and Ascension frame the feeling of a lifeline for the Spirit that moves through each of us, seeking expression.

This book outlines Her light-line. The Sacred Feminine qualities of nurturing, nourishing, acknowledging, accepting, supporting, and cherishing are critical to the world's survival. Here are Her energetic tools for their support. Letting these qualities flow through what is tender, respectful, and sustainable is needed to balance this world at this time.

If you are *done* with the lack of respect for what gives and sustains life, this book is for you.

About the Oneness

When we talk about Oneness, we begin with nature. We start with a reverence for all of life. In general, humans have been conditioned to bury and deny their inherent connection with the natural world, and, therefore, their true nature. And yet, some remember. Some of us *know*.

Reverence is not only about spending time in and with nature, listening to the trees and creature beings, but allowing naturally occurring empathy for all of life to resurrect within us.

Her Oneness simply *is*. It is the nature of this universe and the multiversal realities making up Her infinite field. We are all both wave and particle, fractals of Her field.

Finding the Great Mother

Is She female? Not in the ways we anthropomorphize divinity. She is the Source of All That Is. And, by whatever name She has been called, and there are so very many, She is always present. She is Presence. Present in all forms, male and female, winged, finned, four-legged, the vegetable and mineral kingdoms, and, yes, the bipeds.

We are each a facet of Her jewel. We each have a unique and precious tidbit of Her wisdom to become and to share. This gift is not found anywhere outside of ourselves, though it may be mirrored there. When introspection delves deep enough, there we find Her.

Practicing devotion to our higher power, we acknowledge the divinity in ourselves, others, and the sacredness of life. Why would we want to live any other way? Why have we? And what have we become?

What might we now become?

Introduction

Becoming Oneness is the Sacred Feminine path *through* Enlightenment and into embodying the essence of All That Is. It is the way of total transformation. And it is not only *one way*. The Great Mother is Infinite in Her diversity.

The path to Enlightenment, long a privilege accorded only to men, is one of egoic dissolution and transcendence, or resurrection. What we know ourselves to be must dissolve so we can become something *more*. A caterpillar is not a butterfly. Her way of transcendence is a path of state-shifting from one form of being into another.

As I moved through the various stages of awakening, I asked of Source how I might be of service. I did not come naturally to what is called the service of the Goddess. I had mother issues, woman issues, and was faced with these over and over again, until, finally, She helped me to dissolve enough of my cauterized emotional barriers to feel Her truth.

Introduction

One day, as I read a fantasy novel, I found myself literally on my knees, sobbing, my heart pierced in a way I could not explain. I implored the Great Goddess, the Creatrix of us all, in the words of the novel. "If you will have me, I will serve you."

I recalled other words from other stories into which I had flung myself, unable to cope with my levels of sensitivity and empathy in a world that seemed to value neither. "If you still want so poor a thing, it is yours." ~ quoted from *A Rose in Bloom* by Louisa May Alcott. **Herein lies the enlightened woman's dilemma.**

We have been taught we are too "poor a thing" to merit the light that is our birthright, the love that created us. We rebel and rage against this lie, and yet our conditioning makes it almost impossible to transcend. And so we comply or fight, most often both, and mostly against an unseen enemy within.

The journey home to Her is a journey through the heart, whether we are male or female, and is *the only doorway* through which we can now access awakening. An ego still holding fixed positions can no longer pass this portal. This fact is the true meaning of the camel, or property of a "rich man" that will not fit through the needle's eye.

No enlightenment, no full awakening, is ever the same as any other. Each one is unique, in the way that each Monarch butterfly or Luna moth is unique. Though two may bear similar markings and, to the untrained eye, might seem identical, no two particles of the whole that is Her wave are ever the same.

Becoming Fluid ~

Enlightened Ascension through the Sacred Feminine

What does it mean to become flow?

Ask the caterpillar. As beings in human bodies, we embody the larva stage of spiritual development. We crawl around, feeding ourselves and reproducing, entertaining ourselves along the way.

To become a butterfly, the caterpillar weaves a chrysalis around itself, within which to liquefy. We build a life, a set of circumstances around ourselves, to protect us as we dissolve who we were to become the being we have chosen to be. We do this over and over.

Rigid beliefs, no matter how they may have served us, are the antithesis of life. Life and its energies continuously change. So must we.

This is Her instruction on letting go, releasing, getting rid of the fixed forms of your old reality, and how the old world is coded into you. It is Her way of moving into higher frequencies and a more fluid experience of reality.

How is an Enlightened Embodiment like Becoming a Butterfly?

As with the life cycle of a butterfly, the awakening stages proceed in a natural sequence that cannot be forced. Enlightenment cannot be earned nor conferred. No one can wave a magic wand and give you the Enlightenment or Ascension you desire. If that were possible, every awakened one would have gifted it freely, over and over again. When you reach that stage of spiritual maturity, you will see, feel, and know that this is so.

> A butterfly goes through what is known as complete metamorphosis.
> So, too, does an awakening being.

The four stages of a butterfly's life cycle are egg, larva, pupa, and adult. The butterfly begins life as a round or cylindrical egg. A human body begins life as an egg as well. What we aren't taught about is the energy egg or orb of light surrounding the physical egg, containing it, and nurturing its development. This energy field contains what some call past-life memories and the wisdom that will be helpful in a given life for the lessons we have chosen to learn in this lifetime.

The Enlightenment process is said to take "ten thousand lifetimes," an expression widely misinterpreted to mean literal births, deaths, and rebirths in a human body. A journey into enlightened embodiment can happen this way, yes. More often, many "lifetimes" are lived within one incarnation, especially when we quantum-play and bring alternate realities into the mix.

We are all part of Source, the All That Is. The process of becoming fluid, becoming enlightened or ascended, or whatever terminology best suits you, is a process of embodiment. We must nurture our bodies with the higher frequencies of life-love-light, recognize that they have always been present within us, and let them take over.

Do the body of the caterpillar, and the body of the butterfly exist at the same time? No. One morphs into the other. As long as we are part of a given incarnation, we are subject to its structures and the laws that govern them, until we become fluid.

Becoming more fluid allows you to move into new cycles, new realities, with more ease and grace, finding 'home' within much more quickly, dissolving old programming that exists in fixed forms into alignments that resonate with the vibrations of Divine Truth.

There is only one Divine Truth, and that is Oneness.
We each experience it differently as we grow.

The Great Mother is the flow that guides this transformation.

The Orb of Light

First, we opt-in to an egg. Not only a physical, embryonic structure but the luminous egg that will guide our journey. We gather together our agendas, agreements, preferred archetypal roles, costumes, stage sets, and props. We then choose a family situation that will best help us achieve our incarnation's agendas. These parameters form the foundation of our experience of reality and our ego.

As we develop, physically and mentally, even in utero, our orb of light radiates attraction patterns that pull in data, in the form of character traits, physical attributes, and circumstances in support of our design parameters.

In many lifetimes, we have remembered what we chose and why. Once incarnated, we honed, refined, and often altered our lifetime agreements, parameters, and filters to better express what we had incarnated to become.

In this world, at this time, one of our initial parameters was to forget what we are and why we made our choices in the first place. The challenge is to overcome that forgetting and morph in place, amid familial and collective convictions about what is possible. Unfortunately, incoming data from the world at large acts like reinforced concrete, weighing down and solidifying our conditioning, creating a fixed sense of self, life, and purpose.

How could a butterfly exist, if the caterpillar insisted on its identity?

A striped caterpillar produces a striped butterfly or moth. Why would a caterpillar ever change its stripes? How might that happen? Impossible, or so we are taught to believe. An old cliché states that a leopard cannot change its spots. In a fixed world, that might be true. This world is not fixed. So why do we believe this is so?

All the points of view you have ever held or navigated from; the roles you have identified with and used to describe who you are, habits of behavior, all the ways you defend your limitations. All the ways you might say: "I AM this, I AM not that, or "This is just the way it is." These are fixed positions of identity, like the genetically designed striped patterns and cellular composition of a caterpillar.

When a caterpillar dissolves, it liquefies into a mass of DNA templates, whose striped patterns translate into those of the butterfly or moth it becomes. What stripes would you choose to keep? What could melt away? How would you know what to choose?

Feeding the Sense of Self

When the caterpillar hatches, it eats. Absorbing nutrients and growing are its functions. We do the same; as our bodies grow, our neocortex {thinking brain} develops, and we absorb the information that will assist us in getting through life.

First, we build an ego. We do this by aligning what we learn with our internal agreements and those we incarnate into, such as familial, racial, tribal, national, and geographic norms. We begin to set up structures that revolve around "I am this," and "I am not that." Most of this happens unconsciously.

If we use the famous iceberg analogy, almost all of these definitions navigate below the waterline of life. The caterpillar would call these instinctual patterns and behaviors, if it stopped eating long enough to think about what it was doing. We are taught to look, learn, and habituate ourselves to our environment in the same way. And, so, our ego develops as a survival program.

> Most people survive. Few genuinely live and thrive.

As we live and grow, we build our cocoon. It contains our egoic structures *alongside* what will allow them to dissolve.

A newly hatched caterpillar immediately begins to eat the leaf it clings to, much as a newborn human must suckle. In the caterpillar's case, the mother butterfly instinctively lays her eggs on the type of leaf the caterpillar needs. Each species of caterpillar eats only certain kinds of leaves and is vulnerable at birth, so needs to hatch on the right leaf. The mother butterfly instinctively lays her eggs on the type of leaf that best nurtures the caterpillar.

Caterpillars need to eat voraciously to grow quickly. When a caterpillar is born, they are tiny. When they start eating, they instantly begin to grow and expand. Their exoskeleton (skin) does not stretch, so they grow by "molting" (shedding the outgrown skin) several times as they reach their full size.

Our bodies may mature differently, but we go through a similar process of expansion. As the caterpillar ingests nutrients and environmental data from leaves, we ingest what surrounds us. This data is not limited to physical nutrients, but contains emotions, ideas, and ways of perceiving life.

We choose the environment we will be born into, as much as possible, to ensure our optimal nourishment and nurturing. We do this, knowing we will take the pill of forgetting, and be born into the challenge of remembering and resurrecting.

Why is Creativity a Necessity?

Evolution requires creativity. How could it not? There are set patterns for certain embodiments, and there are agreements holding those in place. There are options available for those wishing a change of stripes, and there are potentials and possibilities available for those who choose a total morph in place. The Universe is infinite in Her possibilities.

Becoming conscious in our creativity alters our internal structures, which is then reflected in our experience of an outer world.

The Nature of Our Agreements

The structure of our bodies and our consciousness comes from a series of agreements we make prior to incarnating and those we make throughout our lifetimes.

A butterfly agrees to the life cycle that will create it, including the egg, type of leaf the egg adheres to, and the kind of caterpillar that emerges. These agreements set in motion the reproductive process that will result in its particular egg being laid, lay the groundwork for the egg being fertilized, hatching into a caterpillar, and so on.

Agreements are set in place as part of the egg and caterpillar stages. An egg lands on the type of leaf that nourishes that particular species of caterpillar. So, our developing bodies gestate in a framework within which they can grow. Our awareness is tied into this framework by a series of agreements.

You can see the tiny caterpillar growing inside if you look closely enough at some moth and butterfly eggs. The eggs vary in shape, depending on the type of butterfly or moth.

The shape of our ego depends on the properties inherent in our fertilized human egg, as well as what we have internalized as part of our learning and growing process. It is important to remember, as Dr. Bruce Lipton writes, "Here is the amazing thing: the caterpillar and the butterfly have the exact same DNA. They are the same organism but are receiving and responding to a different organizing signal." — Bruce H. Lipton, *Spontaneous Evolution: Our Positive Future.* This is where our agreements come into play. They send a network of signals to our DNA, imprinting, implanting, and altering the very structures of our bodies and lives.

All of our internal programs are based on agreements. Some we actively choose. Some we inherited, genetically or through our parents' agreements, similar to the patterns that govern the behavior of the caterpillar. You could say those come standard on the vehicle, whether we find them useful or not, like the ubiquitous cigarette lighter in a car. Interface ports have now replaced many, but this feature used to be standard.

Our agreements form rules and the programs and patterns that enforce them. Each line of code, or instruction to do or be something, or not to do or not be something, creates and supports a code of conduct or habit of behavior. There are conditions for each of these instructions as well. They have triggers and timings for when each direction should be given or executed and how the resulting scenarios are supposed to play out. A caterpillar's inner nature dictates when it has grown enough and molted enough, and it is time to build the cocoon or chrysalis. Our agreements, our contracts, work the same way.

Our minds run on programs based on rules, whose foundations we have agreed to build our bodies and lives upon. All or most of this is unconscious, run by the subconscious mind.

The real drivers, or roots of our core personality and egoic structures, lie in the unconscious mind. How does one access the unconscious?

There are many paths available. Finding a self-inquiry system that leads you to the root cause of self-limiting situations and behaviors is the most common.

The Divine Mother's way goes straight to the heart of the matter. Straight to the heart of *matter*, in fact. What matters is what manifests.

Most of the awakening process happens by freeing the conscious mind of its habituated patterns and the subconscious mind of its conditioned responses, making what is unconscious, conscious.

Emily studied many methods of egoic dissolution. What unlocked her enlightenment was the Great Mother's love. Emily learned that freedom happens through the heart.

What is an Agreement?

Agreements form the foundation of our experience of reality. Lifetime agreements form the parameters by which we move through an incarnation. Subsequent agreements form our egos and personality structures. We make these agreements as a result of past-life experiences, karmic imprints, lifetime agendas, and our childhood conditioning.

Which agreements matter most?
Where is your focus? What we focus on, we become.

Starting with the Personality

One example of a trauma-induced agreement is the burned child. Emily pushed, shoved, and dragged the red bench from under the kitchen table. As she inched closer to the stove, the pan of boiling water looked bigger and bigger. Climbing onto the bench, Emily braced herself against the lip of the stovetop. She ignored how warm it felt because her prize was in sight. There, bobbing away in the boiling water, were her bottles. She was thirsty and wanted some milk. Too young and determined to understand consequences, toddler Emily reached for a bottle. The pan tipped over, pouring boiling water over her little arm and shoulder.

When Emily's screams brought her mother running, she scooped the child up in her arms, trying to comfort her, not knowing what to do about the pain. Emily's father had the presence of mind to call the paramedics, while chiding her mother for not watching out for her.

This event set a nest of programs into motion.

Belief systems: Heat is dangerous. Hot is bad. Mother can't protect me and doesn't know how to help my pain. Father gets things done. The remorse both parents feel is my fault. They're angry at me. Emily's mind and emotions felt those things. Her body chose to understand: *Anger is heat internalized.*

Physical Conditions: Thermal stress. Inflammatory immune and auto-immune responses.

Avoidance pattern: Protect yourself from heat and hot things. They burn.

Stored Dissonance: Trauma, Toxicity, Thought patterns carved in stone for survival.

The anatomy of archetypal burned child trauma is: The child touches something hot for the first time and pulls their little hand back from the heat in shock. Or a parent filled with fear grabs the child away from the heat. Either reaction can create an avoidance pattern in the child's subconscious mind.

If the child is burned, she experiences the trauma *and* the fear of it happening again. The child then embeds an unconscious agreement in cellular memory to avoid the experience of burning. A reinforcing contract is set in place to prevent the trauma from happening again. The body's cellular databanks then seek corroborative evidence.

Are there genetically remembered experiences about fire or heat that will reinforce the new fear and avoidance pattern? Or, is what just happened the result of similar patterns already embedded in the child's cellular matrix? This is the chicken and the egg question. Which came first? If your goal is clarity and fluidity, does it matter? What is important is to clear the causal structures from your body, mind and emotions.

An example corollary agreement might be, "I will never touch the stove again," so later in life, food preparation becomes an issue, but the person never understands why. The child could also subconsciously agree to dislike heat or fire, leading to later physical phobias or inflammatory symptoms. The adult could have an irrational fear of being burned, or this experience could trigger past-life memories of being burned at the stake, which may or may not have happened.

In Emily's case, her body internalized a thermal stress pattern. She grew up with a low tolerance for hot weather, saunas, and steam rooms, and became vulnerable to heatstroke and inflammatory conditions. She took these symptoms for granted until her developing awareness brought them to the fore.

Was the childhood incident with the boiling water responsible for her thermal stress patterns? She didn't know. It certainly was a setup for a lifetime of reactivity. But, was it causal?

We choose past-life records to bring in with us in the same way we choose our parents. These memories are not always our own. One more reason to let them go!

Emily's example is a simple one. Most of our agreements are much more complex and pertain to broader life issues than whether to touch a hot stove or not. All unconscious agreements function in precisely this way, no matter how complex or simplistic they might be.

There are many levels of agreement. In Oneness work, we ask for the root or core agreements to vibrate within us to recognize them and allow Source to dissolve them from the deepest possible place. This dissolution frees us from the myriad symptomatic repercussions of limiting constructs that block us from living our light. Recognizing our agreements allows us to release them.

What About Lifetime Agreements?

A lifetime agreement is a parameter or filter for life experience in a particular incarnation. It is a barrier we will not cross in our lifetime unless we choose to transcend it. These agreements form the rules we live by, formatting what we are here to be, do, and have. The rules run us, unconsciously. They are our autopilot, or default code. We make them or allow ourselves to be imprinted by them, for all kinds of reasons.

We make most of our lifetime agreements to provide us with the experiences we incarnated to have. Sometimes we make these agreements in response to the experience of trauma—the more intense the experience, the stronger the agreement.

As infants, we make thousands of these agreements daily or even hourly as we experience and define the world around us.

Many of our agreements are assimilated from our parents as genetic imprints, or from geographic, national, or tribal allegiances. Most are unconscious for our entire lives.

We make these agreements to define and label the world around us, explain our experience, and find our place within it. Our agreements, taken as a whole, make up our perception of life, how life functions, and how we must function therein. Without a set of agreements in place, our incarnation would have no framework.

When we move into Oneness, we release the agreements that limit us to a particular set of experiences. We can release as many or as few as we choose.

Fear-based agreements are our primary targets for dissolution. Some of our love-based commitments and contracts have to go as well, but only those rooted in fear of loss or gain.

A shock-based agreement works like a legal document, based on protecting assets and avoiding loss. A fear-based agreement protects this commitment like a sub-clause. It contracts us around the original agreement to protect it, like an armadillo curling up inside protective armor.

To work with our issues, we call shock-based agreements commitments (because they are usually stronger), and we call fear-based agreements contracts (because they cause a contraction or armoring of some kind).

Commitments and contracts, or shock and fear-based agreements, are the foundations of our personality programming. When you are ready to let go of something, you can process the commitments and contracts that hold your programming in place. Do so, and the whole architecture of the program you are working with will collapse, along with the core

The Nature of Our Agreements

agreements you uncover. Blast the foundation, and the building collapses along with it.

The process of moving into fluidity and Oneness is releasing all fixed positions, attachments, and aversions in consciousness. It takes a lifetime. It's why we are here. Our egoic structures are a collection of agreements. Some are beneficial. Many are not. It is a waste of energy to judge or blame or feel shame over these internal structures. It is most useful to simply observe them and move the energy, releasing ourselves into more authentic alignment.

All structures are constructed of layers, as most of us know. The deepest layer of any process is the foundational agreement made at the program's inception. Core agreements are a response to the shock and shattering that occurs during original imprinting. We differentiate from Source to have a lifetime of experiences, and the feelings of tearing away or being pushed out of Oneness shape what we become. Reaching and recognizing the inception point of our agreements is sometimes called enlightenment. As we move toward our inception point, we process through our many layers of emotion, releasing as we go.

This base level of shock is an extremely uncomfortable, enervating vibration. It feels like wanting to "jump out of your skin." When this happens, our nerves are sending out an overload signal: too much current. Sometimes the overwhelm is too much dissonance. It can also be too much coherence or resonance, depending on our programming. Have you ever met someone who seemed allergic to love? Might there be parts of you in this kind of avoidance?

The enervating response comes from the vibration of a range of emotions trying to cover up the shock experience. Violating, or entering into proximity of a self-programmed electric fence, sets off our body's alarm system.

When conflicting emotional charges are present simultaneously in the body, as a mask or cover-up for shock, the frequencies vibrate against one another and literally "rub each other the wrong way." When this happens during processing, we know we've "hit a nerve." We're close to a cathartic release.

Contracts act like armoring around commitments, protecting them from discovery, and obligating the program to function. Our commitments and contracts constitute the rule-base we will live by for the rest of our lives until we excavate and dissolve them.

Once we have our personality structure, our rule-base, our conscious minds not only live within that structure, but they also add to it and argue for its existence. An example of this is belief systems. Belief systems are usually layered on top of or enmeshed with contracts.

A belief system is, pure and simple, a thought pattern that has benefit. Your programming argues for a thought pattern, so it becomes a belief system, literally "words to live by."

Thought patterns are the surface layer of programming in our personality structures, the tapes in your head. The repeating stories you're so used to that you ignore them until you get pushed—patterns of thinking that are habitual and resist change. Emotions and habits of behavior reinforce these patterns.

Agreements, belief systems, and thought patterns do not sit separately, one on top of the other like a layer cake, but are interwoven, like the different colored threads in tapestry patterns or the weave of a basket. Emotional charges interpenetrate ALL the layers, right down to the roots.

The Layers of Agreements: {How they hold on}

Construct	Definition	Emotional Patterning
Thought Patterns	A thought pattern can be most easily recognized as one of the 'tapes' that runs in your head all the time. Patterns of thinking that are habitual and resist change.	Thought patterns are reinforced by emotional patterns or habits of behavior.
Belief Systems	A belief system is a thought pattern that you argue for. It has some perceived benefit, according to your programming.	Belief systems are also reinforced by emotional patterns or habits of behavior.
Contracts	Contracts sit on top of or wrap themselves around commitments like armoring. They act like a protective shield holding the commitments in place and protecting them from discovery.	Contracts are constructed of fear / terror, often with anger / rage layered in with or on top of the terror.
Commitments (Core agreements)	Commitments are the root of all personality structures.	Commitments are made in response to the shock of some form of original imprinting of trauma.

The process of becoming Oneness is to find a window into your unconscious at the deepest possible level and to clear your personality structure from its roots. Why not see the vibration of the core agreement and release it from the bottom up?

Are there deeper levels than these structures? Yes! There are levels of agreement, parameters that act like overlays to our basic universal principles (Sacred Law) like the Law of Attraction.

Say you have a limiting agreement that triggers every time you try to activate the Law of Attraction. This overlay filters, or re-directs your conscious intention and attracts what it is programmed to attract, rather than your intended manifestation. This re-direct is why practicing the Law of Attraction without doing deep work gets mixed results. The fastest way to shift your attraction patterns is to find and remove your programming at its roots—at the deepest level possible. Then, your authentic essence is doing the attracting, instead of your limitations.

Sometimes you can go right to your deep agreements or commitment. Sometimes your contracts are so heavily armoring your commitments that you have to find and release the contracts before your unconscious allows you to see what you are protecting. Sometimes you have to clear layers of belief systems, thought patterns, and emotional charges to get to your contracts or commitments. Keep at it! Her clarity and grace await your presence.

Processing your agreements requires a committed intent on your part and the full participation of your intuitive faculties. Releasing commitments and contracts is not difficult, however, and usually produces results in an amazingly short amount of time. The determining factor for success is the amount of committed intent you bring to the work.

Are you ready to shift into a new experience of reality? A more ascended state? If so, the process unwinds itself as fast as your will and Her Grace allow. Remember, these are only programs. Your programs are not who you are, and any program is replaceable.

You do not need to identify with these agreements, although they are programmed to make you believe them. Don't judge your programming. It was put in place to serve you. The *only* issue is that these patterns were put in place by the little self to serve itself. Your Spirit longs for something else. It yearns to be free.

Change your deepest agreements, and you literally change your mind. Change your mind, and you alter your perception of reality.

The Nature of Our Agreements

"If the doors of perception were cleansed, everything would appear to man as it is, Infinite. For man has closed himself up, till he sees all things thro' narrow chinks of his cavern." ~ William Blake

As you observe a situation, ask yourself, "What did I agree to for this to be occurring?" You may find a few layers of vows, oaths, pledges, alliances, and allegiances before you get to the root. I always check for all of the above. Why leave splinters behind?

It also helps to ask, "What is Source showing me? Why did I choose to learn this way?" And, finally, "What is the root of this pattern?" (It will *rarely* be what you thought it was.) Remember, this is a program doing its job. Blaming and raging at our agreements never helps. Be patient with your programming as you optimize its design.

Ask intuitively, and you will see what you need to see. Allow your core to be released back to Source, and you will be free to be who you choose to be.

The Great Mother's perception is available to us all. Through Her eyes, we can learn to perceive clearly, and with gratitude, from the heart.

Dumping Unnecessary Data

In the esoteric spiritual traditions, Buddhism, in particular, emphasis is placed on acquired wisdom, the accumulation of knowledge. Many of us internalized this practice as a way to keep from backsliding, a reminder so mistakes would not be forgotten. The practice contains a legacy of fear entangled with all we learn and gain.

If a caterpillar did the same, would it become a butterfly?

The big picture is bigger than what we believe.

Emily walked along the edge of the nearby lagoon, letting the Earth perform her sorting and reorganizing functions on way too much internal data. As she walked along, watching her internal database reorganize, her perspective widened. She saw infinite wisdom as Infinite. How would she ever internalize all of that?

Dumping Unnecessary Data

Stopping in her tracks, Emily felt the weight of all the learning, knowledge, and data she carried. She felt the heaviness of her mind, the vast amounts of storage. She felt it in her emotions, weighing down their ability to function in a healthy way. And finally, she felt it in her physical body. The weight of it depressed her. What a cocoon she had constructed! It was like a giant snail shell, made of everything Emily thought she had to carry with her to wake up. How would the light ever shine through *that*?

Rooted in the weight of her perceptions, Emily stood, watching the sunlight play through the lagoon's green-brown ripples. She admired the new yellow-green branches of a nearby weeping willow tree. The graceful ebb and flow of its leaves dipped into the currents, flowing along with them as they shifted. The young tree had grown spherically, rooted in fertile soil, her canopy dropping long flexible trailers into the water. Was she drinking from her roots or her branches? Perhaps both.

And then, realization dawned. The tree was open to receiving spherically, from every direction, the sustenance needed from Source. Everything it received flowed through it, nourishing and shaping as it flowed.

Emily re-experienced the weight of the acquired knowledge she'd been carrying around, juxtaposed against the lightness of the willow's grounded fluidity. Her inner vision opened, showing her Source's Infinite Database. All knowledge, of all that is, was or will be. Source's voice was gentle and kind.

All you need is access. Let go and see.

At that moment, Emily's determinedly curated database dropped. Hard bounce. She felt it melting, dissolving, and flowing away, given back to the Source from which it came. For a long time, Emily stood there, gaping at the tree, the water, and the available immensity. When she noticed her surroundings again, it had begun to rain. Lighter by mountains, Emily skipped back to her car, heedless of who might be watching.

Emily built databases for a living. What she learned that day was that the living flow of data does not need to be stored by anyone. Light is information. It knows what to do, where to go, and what needs to be seen.

How do we let go into HER big picture?

There are as many ways to find Her as there are paths to enlightenment and beings who choose them. What all paths have in common is the dissolution of egoic structures. As Yoda said, "You must unlearn what you have learned." You

Dumping Unnecessary Data

must surrender into knowing that you don't know. There is relief in surrender, as you strengthen your trust muscle in new ways.

Her way is gentler, kinder to our bodies, sometimes more intense, and definitively thorough. Bit by bit, we turn over our belief systems, thought patterns, and habits of behavior to Her. We do the work of breaking habits; good, bad, and merely familiar. We learn to recognize our internalized rule bases of *how things are* and let HER change them.

It all begins with what we originally agreed to, our templates, and agendas for this lifetime. When we recognize our inception points, we can use the energy they hold to create ourselves anew.

Sacred Feminine Enlightenment

She resides within all ways. This is the first confusion to be released.

Surrendering to doing deep inner shadow work eventually leads to personal inner mastery. Ask the butterfly.

There are known phases in the transformation cycle that lead to various levels of mastery, enlightenment and ascension. Most are duality-based, and have been traditionally addressed through some form of the reconciliation of opposites.

The Great Mother's way is inclusion. Finding neutrality between opposing forces is only the first step. Allowing the polarity to dissolve and its energies to be freed is the lifelong, continuing process.

The known phases of egoic dissolution are:

Right and wrong

Family of Origin:
- Masculine / feminine
- Family position
- Acceptable behaviors
- Hidden pathologies
- Genetically held interpretations
- Encountering the psychotic core...

Life and Death
- Cyclic learning through consciousness
- "Death is a stripping away of all that is not you. The secret of life is to "die before you die" and find that there is no death." ~ E Tolle. For Eckhart, the only 'real' death is never knowing who you really are, never understanding your true 'being'.

We go through these phases multidimensionally, shifting pieces of each, until we have become the being we choose to be. Funnily enough, that's when the real work of transformation begins.

The caterpillar feeds itself and grows, until it is a perfect caterpillar. Then, it spins a cocoon or chrysalis within which to transform. It is when we have gotten what we thought we wanted, that Source steps in to show us Her way for us.

Enter Emily

Emily is the poster girl for our journey through transformation. She used to be a caterpillar. Like so many before her, she realized that if she wanted to fly, she had to stop being a caterpillar.

Emily had always been different from those around her. She was highly sensitive and loved to spend time in the trees. One day, lying on a long curvy limb that had surely been grown just for her, she heard a new voice. It rose up through her green world companion, flowed with the creek as it danced among the flowers in the field across the way.

"When you're ready to see, there is work to be done. I will always be with you, as you learn to BE."

Emily's Exit

Emily loved Divine light, from the day she was born. She studied many of the world's enlightenment traditions, finally ordained in three. Then, the Great Mother took over, teaching Emily Her way of transforming, from the inside, out.

Her constant message? *"Everything is all right. You are always taken care of."*

The Heartspace

Initiation

The doorway into higher vibrating realities is the heart. While fluid states of being can be accessed in many ways, activating your unique Heartspace is one of the most optimal.

The Heartspace is your unique piece of the unified field, as an integral part of which, you simply ARE. It is the sanctity of your droplet within the wave of life. As an orb of light emanates from your heart, higher octaves of frequency open up to you.

The Heartspace is a vibrational state of being, not a doing.

The three interconnected sacred spaces you will read about are a gift from Source, in Her form as the Divine Mother. She shares this gift of presence, of being held within the Divinity that is present within us all, ascending into higher vibrations directly through the heart.

The Heartspace

The triple alchemical space was a direct transmission from Source to me when I asked for a shortcut, to process that which was no longer needed and to release my body from having to work so hard. We describe the alchemical container as a sphere within a sphere within a sphere, much like those nested dolls, one inside the other. What is being woven, vibrationally, is an inter-dimensional space. With initiation, this triple space becomes *real*. Welcome to Her transformational orbs of light.

Being held differs from holding space, in that we relinquish our role as the doer and allow Spirit to "do" and provide the "how," while we commit to taking only intuitively guided actions. It is a way of re-balancing energies long-held in hierarchical forms, into reverent equality and unity.

The transmission of this triple set of sacred spaces is multidimensional, optimizing your piece of the unity/quantum field for moving through a world in transition.

The initiation into receiving these spaces is a way to move through transition and turmoil into transformation, within the experience of a flow of Grace.

Even though I sometimes describe these structures as containers, a sphere within a sphere within a sphere, the Heartspace is a fluid, inter-dimensional toroidal form. Think of it as your config file or assemblage point for morphing in place.

The Heartspace

The inner-most sphere of your sacred space forms from an expansion of heart energy. If it helps to think of the physical heart, you can use it, or if the heart chakra resonates with you, that can be helpful. What happens is that your heart resonance begins to radiate outward, past what you normally perceive.

The Heartmath Institute maintains that the human heart's bioelectric field is the most powerful in our bodies. The heart chakra, found in the center of the chest, is considered to be our center or core resonator. The spheres we are envisioning build on these concepts and transcend them.

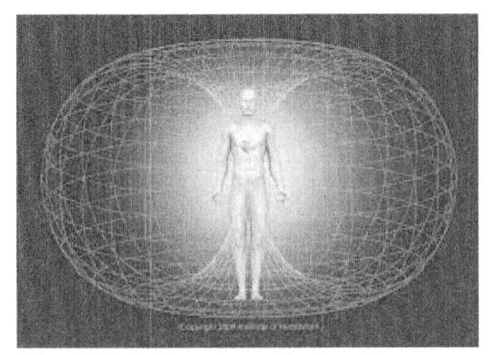

https://elixirultineretii.wordpress.com/7-scientific-reasons-you-should-listen-to-your-heart-not-your-brain/heartmath-institute/

The first, inner-most sphere, comes from an expansion of the heart, as seen in the illustration above. In the twelve-chakra system, there are two heart chakras. Anahata, most commonly known, resides in the center of the chest. The upper heart, the one in the area of the thymus gland, is just above it. Her Heartspace encompasses your physical heart, Anahata, and the upper heart.

How to Visualize the HeartSpace

Bring your attention to the center of your chest. Feel the area behind the breast bone, allowing yourself to experience your heart energy. Place the tips of two fingers against your chest to form an electromagnetic circuit. This circuit acts as a cue to let your body know to center in the heart. Breathe into that space, letting it begin to vibrate.

Allow your experience of this space to enlarge. Don't put limits on how this happens, what it looks like, or how large your sphere becomes. Let yourself rest within the supportive energies of the heart, even as they expand from you.

You may see a point or orb of light, a lotus blossom, or another form that represents these energies. Whatever feels good, safe, and supportive is what is correct for *you.* Let it be beautiful. Let it be powerful. There is no wrong way to perceive this space.

With each breath, allow the point of light in the center of your chest to expand. Allow it to increase in size, spherically, in every direction. Take a couple of big deep breaths in, and, as you release each breath, let your orb of light grow larger.

Breathe normally and continue to expand until the heart sphere is large enough to encompass your physical body. One of the most recognizable illustrations of this sphere is Da Vinci's Vitruvian Man. In martial arts, they call this the "circle"; the distance your arms and legs reach when stretched out. The Heartspace, however, becomes more extensive than the circle. Let it expand.

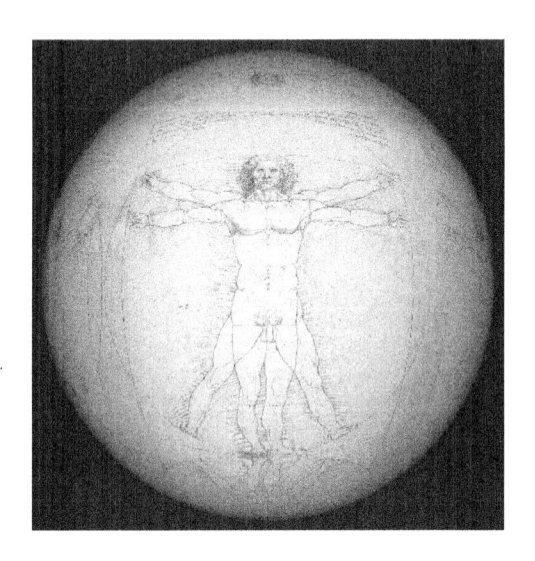

Your entire physical body lives within this sphere of light. It also contains your emotional body, your feeling states, and your various states of mind. It includes the conscious, the subconscious (where we hold belief systems, thought patterns and habits of behavior), and the unconscious mind, which is the portion of our iceberg below the surface of life's waters. Allow all levels of yourself, all agreements, everything you've carried forward in any part of yourself for all of the last cycle, to be held. The Heartspace is big enough to hold it all.

Allow yourself to rest in this *safe*, sacrosanct space. This is the sacred space that you *are*, whether you recognize it yet or not. The sacred space is the particle, which is your unique expression of Divinity within the wave. *The Heartspace expresses both the particle and the wave, from a particular perspective.*

Allow this sphere to expand around you into a beautiful orb of light, a lovely bright ball. You can think of it as a clear crystal that has surrounded you, whose energy is entirely flexible, morphable, and filled with particular energies. These energies nurture, nourish, support, acknowledge, appreciate, and cherish *you,* the Divinity that *you* are.

These energies are the essence of the Great Mother. Being held is a gift from her. She holds us through the turmoil of life's transitions, allowing transformation to become a flow of ease and Grace. It is a gift beyond measure.

These qualities, the essence of the Great Mother's heart, are Source's definitions, not the ego or the mind's definitions. She offers us Her currents, Her waves within which to flow.

Understanding the Heartspace

Now that you've visualized your Heartspace, it's time to get to know it. This space is your sacred and unassailable sanctuary. It is your center for wellness, healing, and divine love.

The specific qualities of the Heartspace are those that nourish, nurture, acknowledge, accept, appreciate, support, and cherish *you.* Here, the individuated heart becomes one with the heart of the Divine Mother.

Nourish

How *does* the energy of nourishing feel to you? What nourishes your spirit, your body? What feeds every part of you? If you're ready, commit to allowing yourself to receive more of that nourishment, as much as the Great Mother can provide. Release any fears of overwhelm, because what She offers will be a lot!

Then, invite *anything* that is *pretending* to nourish you into the chrysalis. For example, "I always thought that worked for me," or "I always liked that," or similar thoughts with different flavors. Let all old ideas of nourishment be moved into the protective layer around you and observe how they shift. When that feels complete, meditate on the resulting peace and safety. When you're ready, summon the energies of nurturing.

Nurture

Ask yourself this: What nurtures my essence, my spirit, and my heart? What uplifts me? What inspires me? You're asking for essence, for feeling, although you may receive images, sounds, or words. Steep in the warmth of nurture like a teabag. Let yourself soak. Then, ask, what is *pretending* to nurture me, or is now an obsolete form of nurturing that no longer resonates? To those energies that surface, simply say, "thank you" and send them into the chrysalis. They may be costumes, stage sets, props, or archetypes. Whatever shows up, release it. Let it go.

Support

One of the key issues in feminine spirituality is support. The Great Mother has been disenfranchised and we, along with Her.

Allow yourself the *experience,* in whatever way it shows up, of how unconditional support from the Divine Mother feels. Allow yourself to experience the place where She not only has your back but your front, your top, your sides, your *everything.* She is unreservedly holding *every* aspect, every particle of you. How does it feel? *Allow* it, receive it. Ask! And see what she offers for you to receive.

If there is any part of you that tells you, "I don't know if that works, it's never worked before," you are hearing the voice of resistance. *It denies your Divinity.* How could a particle of the Divine not be worthy of the wave? How could a piece of the Divine be undeserving? What grander load of garbage could we have been handed?

We did it to ourselves by choosing to experience an incarnation of separation. That choice doesn't matter anymore. Remember that what matters manifests, and choose again! It is time to learn immersion in real support.

Are there any vibrations within your Heartspace telling you they support you, but they don't? They know it's their job, but how these pieces function is not supportive anymore. Separation from Source is an example of one of these structures of lies. Inappropriate boundaries, or the lack of them, is another. As a particle of love, you need healthy boundaries. As with your intentions, so with your cells and physical systems.

There is confusion in the world around boundaries, separation, and unity. The first thing to remember is that these are *words*. Words symbolize thoughts and feelings, creating structures of vibration, and are therefore important. Words are not, however, anything other than symbols of energy. It may help you to know that.

Her unified field contains all waves, all particles, and is separate from none. Anything *in particular* self-perceives as individuated, as unique within the waves. That uniqueness requires boundaries, permeable to *Source*, and not to that which is toxic to the sacredness within.

What is the real essence of support, and what parts of your life have been faking it? Don't judge what you see. Change your internal dialogue. Ask your mind to listen to Her heart. At some point, your mind will bow to your heart, and all of your cumulative changes will coalesce into unity.

Acknowledgment

How do you feel when your core essence is acknowledged? When you are recognized for all of your gifts, talents, and light? How does acknowledgment feel? What about the parts of you that represent a crunchy work in progress? Don't they need recognition as well? The Tibetans have a saying, "Recognition is Liberation." What we recognize, we can release or set free.

Let your mind stop pretending it knows what to do. That is mostly ego. It may have collected data along the way, but the world is changing, so the mind's accumulated data has lost value. Let those databases go. Send them home. Let your mental body release its storehouse. The Divine Mother is Infinite. So is her wisdom. All you need is good data access. She will show you as you learn to allow.

You don't need to carry a burden of knowledge anymore. So, again, observe which energies are pretending to be acknowledgment. What parts of you believe they acknowledge you or attract acknowledgment, but the belief is a lie? Lip service of every kind must go into the chrysalis. We no longer have the luxury of paying lip service to our core essence. Let Her show you the frequencies of true acknowledgment.

Acceptance

Acceptance of every part of ourselves is crucial to full awakening. As tolerance is the first step towards anything that doesn't resonate, acceptance is the key that releases self-judgment and the judgments we project onto others.

Using the sanctuary of the heart, we can look through divine eyes at whatever comes. The Great Mother's perceptual array goes far beyond old cycle concepts of neutrality, useful though they have been, and into the frequencies of Mother-Love for every aspect of life. This perspective is most beneficial as we learn to view what our egos, or anyone else's, have been up to, with dispassion and courtesy, if not compassion and kindness.

Ask for acceptance and see where Her perspective leads you.

Appreciation

What is the vibration of appreciation for the Divinity that you are? You have to feel it before the world will reflect it to you. You can't receive the reflection until you embody the vibration. So, how does deep, inner appreciation feel? **It's a love affair between the particle and the**

wave. Let yourself feel that for as long as you like. Immerse yourself in the intimacy and shared love of all parts of Divinity for Herself.

What energies within you *tell you* they appreciate you, but do not? They tried, but how these energies function no longer works with your ascending vibration. These programs are obsolete. Don't hate them. Speak to them as a mother would {on a good day} to a child throwing a tantrum. Be as firm or as gentle as you need to be. Say, "Thank you. Well done. Now I'm going to let the Great Mother replace those dying vibrations with the love, the light, the clarity, and the information you need (speaking to the programs) to do your job well."

Egoic programs co-opt your core essence. Core essence is permanent, designed by Source. You are a co-creation, and your interior programs are your core creations. They need to upgrade in a *quantum* way, through Her infinite possibilities. Our world is going through this upgrade. Going through this consciously will help you, giving you a reference for your transformations.

When you can appreciate what is, there is more available Grace for what can be.

Cherishing

Cherishing is not the opposite of being abandoned, rejected, or betrayed. The frequency of cherishing is completeness and wholeness. It is the unconditional embrace of the Divine. Let this vibration fill your Heartspace and relax into it like a soothing bath. Let the Divine that you are, absorb as much cherishing as it can hold.

You are remembering the flow of core essence, shifting into a more expanded core essence. This is how shifting from the heart begins.

There are no imprints, no implants, no lies, no more illusion, no false humility, no false pride, *no false anything*. What is the truth of being cherished? What parts of you are *pretending* to be the truth but only playing the game of truth? All truth is subjective until we have windows into what is REAL.

Subjective truth is okay as long as it is divinely aligned. It's the distorted stuff that is not useful. Notice the difference between the *feeling of being cherished* and the *illusion of being cherished*. Let the illusion go into the chrysalis. Then allow the *entire* relationship between all aspects of you that perceive themselves as you, and all aspects of the Divine that see themselves as separate, move into the chrysalis from every direction. You are an omnidirectional force of light; *that* is true. To the voice that says, "It doesn't look that way in this part of my life," offer that part of yourself a new perspective.

Allow your Heartspace to vibrate with the commitment of having clear, undistorted windows. It's time for truth.

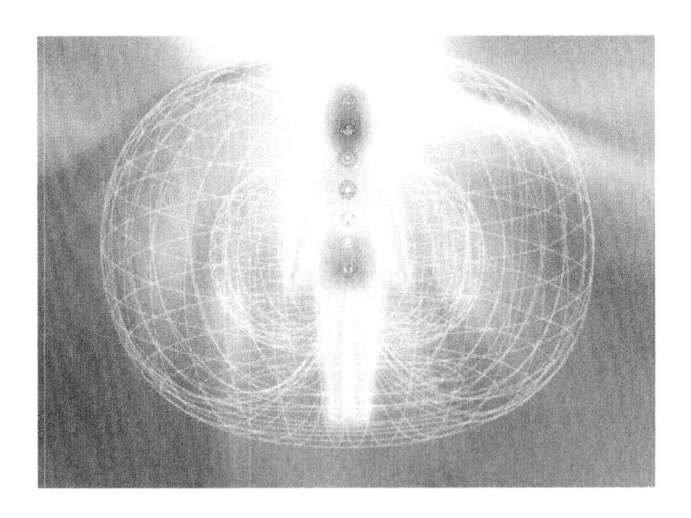

The Chrysalis

Awakening accelerates when we begin to build a sacred space within which to transform. First, we build a cocoon, an opaque container for our growth and development. As we dissolve and awaken, our container changes. It becomes transparent, as we do.

The cocoon surrounds the Heartspace, forming a thick energy boundary larger than the Heartspace, yet permeating it. As we shift, the opaque, cocoon-like sphere reveals its true function as a torus of increasing clarity.

The chrysalis becomes the butterfly's protective container, while its old life as a caterpillar dissolves. Our cocoon or chrysalis works the same way.

Butterfly medicine is that of transformation. The metaphor of the caterpillar is all of our old identities and ways of being. The chrysalis is the Great Mother's tool for dissolving all of those people, archetypes, and roles we have believed ourselves to be.

The world is awakening. It's time for you, the caterpillar, to move into your cocoon, dissolve the opacity, reconfigure through the chrysalis and become something more.

The Newly-Awakening

The in-between process from caterpillar to butterfly appears chaotic, confusing, and disorienting. What needs to happen is a breakthrough, though that can seem impossible.

In nature, the caterpillar dissolves completely. Does it feel like death to the caterpillar? We don't know. Does it instinctively trust this process? Yes, it does, or it would not build the container. Many caterpillars become distracted from eating and growing, become food for predators, or wither due to harmful environmental influences. So do many who might awaken.

Dissolution is part of a caterpillar's cycle, part of its process. And so, part of the Divine Mother's gift is this cocooning energy, where we can dissolve, liquefy, transform, and embody fluidity in Her flow of grace.

Many of our energy patterns *have the potential* to align with higher frequencies but have not yet made the jump. Some of our old programs tell us they're being helpful but are often doing the opposite. Sometimes, these energies are hidden forms of fear, pretending not to be afraid, and occasionally these patterns are deeper and darker than fear and make us afraid of them.

All transformation can happen in the Cocoon/Chrysalis, instead of detoxing through the physical body. This container becomes the vehicle for change. It takes *over* from the physical body, providing a flexible, fluid safety.

Invite any suspect energies to move into the chrysalis.

Some people prefer the expression, "the Divine Mother's blender," because blender action is how energy moves from opacity and fixed positions into transparency in the chrysalis. It acts as a buffer zone, so your physical body is relieved of the burden of processing difficult energies. Our bodies have done so much! They deserve our love and care, and easeful alignment with Her higher frequencies.

The Heartspace provides a womb of purity, filled with divine light and love. The chrysalis provides the transformative space that replaces your physical body as the purifying vehicle for your programs and patterns.

Becoming Oneness

The Divine Mother has given us these tools, but we must do the work of releasing all agreements, contracts, and vows we've made to process things using our physical bodies and lives. We all sign up for the event-driven school of learning at first, but we can release those agreements and begin to learn through conscious observation.

In these times of transition, our physical bodies can have a rough time of it. Not all bodies will be able to sustain the level of change happening on the planet. So, to ease the physical body's burden, release any agreements you may have that hold you in limitation. It can help to see your programs, patterns, and agreements as lines of code. They are the internal software that keeps your identity in place. Let them all go, if you dare.

As your old scripts dissolve, like the caterpillar's body, it may seem like you're watching the story of your life roll past. As each pattern releases, you begin to feel more fluid. Trust the fluidity! Allow your body to stop carrying around job descriptions defined by obsolete lines of code, once and for all!

As you begin to feel the chrysalis taking over the transformative function, remind your physical body that *no detox is needed. No healing crisis is necessary, and no event-driven learning required for transformation*. Your body no longer needs to use symptoms to get your attention, except in an emergency.

You are moving from the event-driven school of learning to learning through perception, feeling, and consciousness. Learning by perceiving through conscious awareness is much faster, much more efficient, and much more comfortable than the event-driven learning you have grown up with. Learning by immersion in higher frequencies creates a new experience of reality through intention, decision, and commitment. Like anything, it takes practice.

Some aspects of your mind may continue to be troublesome. They may resist, telling you they aren't ready to be transformed. Resistance is a normal part of the process. We have many layers of mental programming, and dissolution happens in layers as well. The release works like an ocean wave, moving in and drawing back out, its ebb and flow matching the tides of the Infinite.

Allow Her energy to wash through your layers and gently pare your consciousness to the core.

Resting in Her Heartspace and using Her chrysalis to transform is the first phase in the transformation process. We invite the authentic SELF into Her heart, escorting all transforming energies into the chrysalis. It begins with our braver aspects and, as we practice, many different parts of ourselves show up. Old relationships, old elements of personality, conditional personality traits, money, and all kinds of things begin to invite themselves into the transformation process. The parade of circumstances is all very normal as the waves of letting go keep moving.

Observe the waves of release until you notice, or She informs you, that you are through to the core of what is holding this layer, archetype, or program in place.

The Reality Construct

The third sphere of Her triple space is the Reality Construct, aka, your life. We've all heard that life is a mirror. The truth is that life's mirror is like a funhouse mirror. It is not a direct reflection, but distorted. The mirror of life is always metaphorical and symbolic. In other words, the mirror of your life experience carries the same kind of distortions that funhouse mirrors do.

Envision a theater in the round. Standing in the middle of the theater, you have a 360-degree view of everything around you. This perspective is the gift of the Reality Construct, including above and below. It encompasses your entire experience of reality. Close your eyes and observe this for a moment. Feel into the larger sphere of your life experience.

We tend to view ourselves as separate from the world around us, moving through it in a linear manner. Instead, feel yourself in the center of a vast sphere of life, whose energies shift and change as you do. It sometimes helps to see this sphere as a disco ball with mirrors facing inwards. What is being reflected, at any given moment, on any given day, in any given experience?

The third container serves two functions; it is the field of your life experience and the reflection of your inner resonance. The Dalai Lama calls this concept "living within the contents of your own mind". The Divine Mother holds the Reality Construct as a reflection of your inner vibration. It is more commonly known as "the Field." If you are quantumly inclined, you will understand that Her field, the infinite domain, is filled with and made up of zero-point energy. It is the "star stuff" that forms the All.

Each of us functions as a fractal of the infinite field. Your fractal works as a feedback loop for what you came into this life to learn and to create. It is a place where you can create your experience of reality in alignment with the Divine as you learn your lessons, and learn to dissolve internalized obstructions to Oneness.

Reality Construct mirrors show us how we are aligned and how our alignment functions. It becomes a reflection of intent, a reflection of our ability to allow and receive, especially receive, and a representation of where we still have distortions and core misperceptions.

As you allow yourself to be held in the Heartspace and allow the chrysalis to function as the transformer, your experience of reality begins to reflect more *clarity* than distortion. You can observe from inner certainty, perceiving from truth rather than egoic misalignment.

As you live in the Heartspace, the chrysalis functions on love speed. The Divine Mother has already pushed the blender button. Anything you've invited into the chrysalis is already transforming. While this is happening, allow life's mirror to show you what is holding truth and what is holding any kind of misperception. The way to approach these reflections is without judgment, without self-criticism, and without blame. Simply observe what is present.

Let these three spheres, one inside the other, *support* you as you transform. The gift of Her sacred space is always present. You are held within it, and you need not step into any other reality. Her sacred space goes with you, whether you are sitting in your office, or on the train, when you take out the trash, when you exercise and when you sleep. She is ever-present! The Divine Mother will never take this away.

Becoming Oneness

With this awareness, you can go deeper into the Heartspace and feel those little places, the *tiny* spots that look and feel like splinters, or thorns—the things that say you can't trust, for whatever reason. You know those voices. There were probably good reasons for them at some point, but they were reactive reasons. When we have a painful place or a little fishhook that always seems to grab at us, it is always reactive. It is not an accurate response, or it would have moved through and transformed because that is what responsiveness does. Responsiveness is fluid. Reactivity is not, and cannot be other than it is.

A reaction gets stuck and defines rules and limitations to defend the stuck place. But you can ask any reactive rules or limitations, no matter how small, no matter how seemingly benign, no matter how seemingly helpful, no matter how large, to go into the chrysalis, either from the Heartspace or from a place of quiet observation or meditation.

Try this when you have a few minutes. Bring your attention to the Reality Construct and observe anything in *that* sphere that feels abrasive or scary. You can see the distortions, though there may be a part of you that doesn't want to look. Let that part be invited into the chrysalis as well. Remember that the chrysalis functions as a buffer zone where *anything* abrasive can shift. Its action is to transform, not to attract poison and transmute; that is a different kind of alchemy.

Transmutation is an old cycle function. What will work going forward is transformation. Allow anything uncomfortable to move into the chrysalis. Feel what aspects of self need to move or are already in motion. What aspects of yourself are moving, changing, and morphing? Have any of your mirrors altered in any way?

Invite your heart's yearnings into your field. Remember, what your heart yearns for, yearns for you. In unity, there is no separation.

Allow your heart's yearnings to move into the reality construct and observe how it transforms. Even if you aren't getting up in the morning and asking the Divine Mother, "How will we play today, what will we dream today?" Even if you haven't ever considered that, take a moment to observe. What is in your reality experience that is mirroring a reflection from your heart's yearnings? These reflections are where your focus needs to be.

What are all the things that are wonderful and special that invite your gratitude? Which ones might be new? What might be showing up that's energetically different? Or maybe something is present that you haven't allowed yourself to have until now. It can be a person, place, or thing. It could be an energy or a state of being. It will be something that you are letting yourself receive, that previously has been problematic. Let yourself see that.

Let the Divine Mother hold up the frame and show you what your heart's yearnings are creating. *Your heart and Her heart are the same.*

If there are any feelings of lack of trust or unworthiness, move them into the chrysalis. As you become more comfortable with these tools, you will find those self-deprecating feelings no longer matter. Let any fear go into the chrysalis and watch as Her love changes the reflections that shape your reality construct and your life.

Being held in the Heartspace is not a doing. So when the mind starts protesting, tell it to be still. Let yourself be held. Let yourself be *absorbed* by Her grace. Let any aspects that are not in alignment with the Heartspace energies move into the chrysalis. You don't need to know what they are. The Divine Mother is the doer here, so anything that is not aligned with the Nourishment, Nurturing, Support, Acknowledgment, Appreciation, and the Cherishing of you, let it move into the chrysalis. Let *Her* move it and let go of control.

Observe the chrysalis, in action, for a minute or so. It looks like a swirling blender or like the funnel cloud of a cyclone. Watch as the energies shift and transform into beautiful light. They always were that beautiful light. They have been trapped in a form that is no longer useful.

Let the obsolete energies be moved by the Divine Mother, *wherever* they need to go. You may see things move into particular aspects of your reality construct, or you may not. You may feel them come back into the Heartspace, or you may not. Let the transformation process happen *around* you, inside the chrysalis. Remind your physical body that any contracts, vows, agreements, or anything in the deep levels of mind that dictate to the body, *no longer need to be obeyed.* Give your physical body permission to *stop listening*. Give it an instruction to let go.

The mind likes to see things as fixed, but you have chosen to be fluid, which might kick up some resistance. Let the resistance go, along with all ideas of rigidity. You don't need to know what they are.

Intend that your resistance is released, and observe. You will see what you need to see, no more, no less. The rest doesn't matter.

Let the chrysalis energies move and simply watch from your safe place in the Heartspace.

As the reality construct shifts, you'll notice that the chrysalis will keep transforming energies for as long as is needed. It functions in real-time. This gift from the Divine Mother is forever. She will never let you go. Your job is to learn to relax into Her. Dropping into the Heartspace is like exercising a new muscle. Let Her do the moving of anything that wants to be seen, acknowledged, and shifted through the chrysalis. All you need to do is issue the invitation.

Emily had a hard time trusting the Divine Mother, and she knew why. Her relationship with her birth mother was complicated and wary. Emily had learned to love her mother from what she called "a safe distance." They were too different, and from Emily's point of view, she was reluctant to open herself up to attack and betrayal.

She was willing to give the cocooning process a try, as she felt she had tried everything before and nothing had helped. As with so many of us, she approached the Divine Mother out of desperation.

As surface emotions and memories shifted, what then came up for her was being unsure if she was worthy to receive the gift of being held by the Divine Mother. Like so many of us, Emily was used to receiving small pieces of what she wanted, not the whole thing. She had become addicted to the breadcrumbs of life and had an internalized fear of the Divine Mother's love.

Little by little, Emily surrendered her lack of trust, her fears, and defensiveness into the Divine Mother's arms. As she learned to let herself be loved, her trust muscle became stronger.

When we are held, the only thing we need to do is act on our intuition, nothing else. At first, we start acting on intuition when we remember to, then we start acting on it as much as we can (except for all the other stuff we think we have to do), and *then* we get to the point where we act only on intuition. Living this way seems paradoxical, as though it doesn't fit in with what everyone calls the "real world." The truth is, it's a way of navigating the world most optimally.

Everything the Divine Mother does is optimal. Everything. When we can surrender into that, our surrender releases a flow of ease and grace.

The Heartspace helps you remember to allow yourself to be held. In this place, separation doesn't exist, duality doesn't exist. Your mind will try to argue. It will bring up anything that contains something *other* than this droplet of the unified field that you are. Don't listen.

We are in a new cycle, a cycle of maturing spirituality. When we mature, we need to let go of childish things. None of the old ways apply, and none of the old ways will work in the way they used to do. We must let go of the memories, all proof, and evidence that says, "I can't ever co-create with the Divine," which is another way of saying, "I can't have what my heart desires." The truth is, *yes, you can.*

For Emily, the primary thing she wanted to put into the chrysalis was her unworthiness to be Divine, to walk her divinity. Regardless of what the funhouse mirrors might be showing any of us, we have to be able to look at them, know that what they are showing is not true, and then offer that up.

We are not separate from Her. We are extensions of Source, appearing to be these individuated, independent beings, but we're not at all.

As an extension of the Divine Mother, how could any part of you be unworthy?

The Setup for Becoming~ Preparing to Spin a Chrysalis

The setup for Becoming Oneness is a threefold set of practices you will use to prepare your consciousness for change. How you choose to implement these practices will be unique to you.

The basics, or foundations for Becoming, are meditation, minding the mind, often called mindfulness or presence, and movement. These foundations give you nourishment and grounding to root out what does not serve you, and safely move into spiritual maturity and ascending frequencies.

You need these practices to help you discern what will assist you in creating sustainable change as you traverse the realities that shape your becoming. Your practice will form an energetic chrysalis, within which to morph and dissolve your egoic patterns.

Meditation

The truth of Oneness is that the Infinite can only guard, protect and honor sanctuary when we create it for ourselves.

Are you familiar with the solitude and sacred space inside you that can assist you in letting go? Are you aware that The Great Mother will hold that space through you if you allow Her to do so?

By learning to inhabit your sacred space, you ground through your authentic roots, opening the gift of your innermost nature. The luminous egg, the orb of light, merkabah, Heartspace, cocoon/chrysalis, and other energetic forms, are all ways of describing inner sacred space.

Do we also require sacred physical space to awaken and ascend? Yes. Absolutely. Especially when we have chosen to become the stillness from which all movement flows.

What is Meditation and Why Does it Matter?

Meditation is taught differently in every enlightenment tradition. In popular culture, meditation often refers to deep relaxation and stress reduction. When any deep spiritual practice goes mainstream, dilution tends to be the result.

The Setup for Becoming

There are many meditation apps available. These apps are, by and large, tools that you can safely and productively use to help you to relax and begin to learn about what brings you peace and presence in the moment. You can listen to the app, get quiet, and release some stress. You may be able to become still and feel better, yes, but that is all you will achieve.

Calming oneself is a beginning. You will need to learn to quiet your mind, calm your emotions, and release your thoughts. These are not true meditative states.

The meditative state is a state of *being* that precedes all others. It is the natural and original state of purity and clarity to which we return when our minds and egos dissolve at physical death, sometimes after a whirlwind tour through some bardo (afterlife boot camp) experiences.

What meditation techniques work best for dissolution into Her Oneness?

No one tradition holds the tech award for this one. There are many proven techniques. One or more will work for you. Your mission, if you genuinely seek to shift your awareness, is to find those that work for you and practice them.

Paying attention to and counting or noticing your breaths is one technique from one tradition. Gazing at a candle flame or yantra {sacred design} is another. The object is to find practices that still your mind. Many of the best, from the Sacred Feminine point of view, involve movement. Yoga, walking meditation, tai chi, and chi gong, are examples. Walking in nature works as well.

If you have tried to meditate and, in your judgment, failed, don't give up! Try focusing on your heart. The heart is the pathway through the Sacred Feminine into the higher realms of light.

Sound can also be helpful. Specific sound waves alter human biology in favor of optimal heartbeat, lowered cortisol {stress hormone}, and increased endorphin production. Chanting a mantra is the traditional application of this technique. Frequencies generated by chanting a mantra tap into endorphin production in the brain, promoting a shift in brain waves to delta or theta. These waves are the threshold of meditative states of being.

The most often used mantra in the world is Aum, sometimes misspelled as Om. Properly sounded, this sacred syllable balances body, mind, and spirit. Its component vibrations are "Ah," the frequency of manifestation, "Ooh," a frequency of connection and conductivity, and

"Ma," heart-opening reverence for the Great Mother.

True meditation is when thought stops ruling your mind. The clearer and more still your mind becomes, the more awareness you embody.

Trying to stop thought is noble, and a mandatory pursuit in some traditions. Most of the people I work with find that an impossible task in this age of constant digital distraction. So let's start with something not so seemingly impossible.

A true meditative state is one in which the mind gives up control, even a little bit, to the Infinite. Eventually, as the ego-mind lets go more and more, meditation dissolves the ego, releases thought patterns and belief systems, and shifts behaviors. This process is traditionally said to take "ten thousand lifetimes." Who has that kind of time in a world gone weird?

What if the meditative state is your birthright and an intrinsic part of you? Would that feel better? It's true.

I am *not* saying that you already know how to meditate and are a natural at it. What I will say is that everyone meditates, most without realizing it.

So you haven't found your way yet. Welcome to beginner's alley. It's the foyer to a magical place of wonder and the doorway to the Infinite.
What will it take to find your way? She has a suggestion.

What do you love? Feel it and answer quickly, without thinking. I repeat, without thought. There. If you dropped into your heart, you just stopped thought for a second. A second is a beginning.

What resonates with you? Music creates and alters worlds, so there will be some form of music somewhere that will move you into that feeling state of love and gratitude. In that feeling state, thought does not exist within the mind because you have moved into an altered state where it cannot originate. That is the first key.

Thoughts can drift in from others' minds, from the TV, your smartphone, and the cell towers whose broadcast bandwidths bombard you every day. Begin with discernment. Be still for a few minutes, even if you have to wear yourself out with some physical activity to achieve stillness at first! I remember my Mum used to make my little brother do laps around the outside of our house to discharge excess energy so he could sit quietly and do his homework. In turbulent

The Setup for Becoming

times, we need to discharge backed-up energy as much as we need to receive what sustains us.

Once you're able to be still, listen to what you're thinking. No one ever wants to do this at the beginning. It is one of the principles of mindfulness, yes, and we'll get to what to do with your thoughts in the next section. First, listen. Now connect the listening to feeling. Does a particular thought resonate with your feeling center? Does it trigger a reaction from you? Or is it part of the white noise you ignore every day? No scorecards. Only observe.

What to do with the observation? Noticing what you *want* to do with a thought or feeling will lead you in the direction of what resonates and what does not. Is this a good feeling, or is it uncomfortable? Noticing what feels good or not is discernment, one of the first steps into a meditative state.

What pulls my attention? What do I ignore? Does something feel 'off' or funny? Ask yourself, your physical body, and Source why you feel this way.

It takes years to eliminate the origination of thought from your mind. You might not think you have that long, so try this instead, just for fun. Offer up your mind, your thinking process, and everything you think you know, have learned, and are learning to Source. Surrender the contents of your mind. Give it all back. The Infinite's database is just that, infinite. You don't need to carry a heavy burden of information around with you. It will be there when you need it.

You will find access to the ALL through your heart, in silence. Inner silence, if not outer. Inner stillness even in the face of the seemingly limitless disgruntled disquiet of the current world.

What makes you feel relaxed, heart-centered, and still? Start there. Let your way find you instead of spending time and energy looking for it.

The polarity of seeker/finder is replaced by becoming an expression of the unified field. In unity, all ways absolutely and unconditionally exist, including yours.

Don't give up before the miracle. Use the tools available to find your most resonant source of SOURCE. Drop into it with everything you are. Begin again, with every practice.

So, what is a deep meditative state? The answer to that question varies. She answers that meditation is a deep, non-reactive presence. A state wherein one is absorbed into Her Infinite

The Setup for Becoming

Field, absorbed into the clear light of reality. Achieving this can take years of practice, though it is a naturally occurring state in infants and nature.

We have all felt the profound peace of the natural world. Nature is our greatest ally in experiencing stillness. Notice that stillness is not without sound. Birdsong, the rustling of the wind through the trees or the lap or crashing of waves, these are all part of Her ever-moving peace. The harmony of nature supports inner stillness. It is the source of all mantras.

When we spend time in nature, we tend to think less. Our minds become quieter. Our thoughts move out of the circus ring of constant performance pressure and into their appropriate functional place. Depending on how our minds have been trained, letting thought find its river bottom takes a lot of patience.

What are your ideas and definitions of meditation? Are there biases involved? Are you biased for or against one form of practice or another? If so, bring these judgments into your conscious awareness and release them in a spirit of humility. Let Her show you what meditation is for you, and how it can benefit your life, balance your body, and clear your mind.

The first step is to allow yourself to receive Her guidance. Be in a quiet, receptive state. You don't have to be sitting still and concentrating. Fierce concentration blocks receiving!

Quietly listen to what your heart tells you. Don't let your mind get in the way. Don't let it recite any litany of "how to meditate" or of any particular practice you may have participated in or imagined. Your mind will always try to help you by dredging up all available data. Your choices throughout your lifetime have built its sorting algorithms.

Your mind will pull up facts or memories it feels will help you in its pre-stored order of importance. When you are shifting consciousness, this is counter-productive, because the data will need to be changed or, at the very least, re-arranged.

Let Her show you what works for you, what is optimal in the present moment. Your meditation practice may vary from day to day.

It is more important to be consistent in cultivating stillness than to have your practice look a certain way. Her way of meditation is receptive.

The Great Mother asks us to relax into stillness, to be absorbed into the light. It is resting in our true nature and what supports us, rather than striving toward some imagined pinnacle. The more we reach for Her in meditation, the more we push Her away. It seems paradoxical, but it is true, especially in higher vibratory states of being.

She asks that we let Her find us and allow Her to show us new ways to be.

Meditation begins the sorting process, where we let go of what no longer serves our expanding consciousness and focus on what benefits us. Becoming more aware is the first step in awakening.

Minding the Mind ~ Mindfulness

The practice of mindfulness is to monitor your environmental intake and change the way your mind and physical body process information. You change the way you think, and how your thoughts affect your brain and physical function. By so doing, you literally change your mind. You begin to function as a piece of Divine Mind.

As the world moves from the age of information to an era of intuition, it benefits us to pay attention to the diet we feed all parts of ourselves. As it is important what we put into our bodies, what we put into our minds is also essential. It is even more important what we allow them to store. What our minds store, and how, forms our habits, beliefs, and how we react to circumstances. This storage silo is like the larger part of an iceberg, not visible above the waterline. This deeper part of us is what navigates life's currents, while our beliefs tell us our conscious mind is in control.

As we mind our minds, being as fully present as possible, we begin to bring what is subconscious and unconscious to the surface of our awareness. The more that surfaces, the more we can let go. The more conscious we are of the contents of our minds, the clearer we become.

You can enhance your life and your attraction patterns by changing your beliefs, thought patterns, and habits of behavior. Change happens as you acknowledge and accept your mind's contents and let go of what does not sustain you.

Caterpillars are essentially "eating machines", gathering and storing up vital nutrients so that their adult forms can develop strong wings, flight muscles and other functional structures. Changes in the quality or quantity of food consumed during the larval stage can directly affect the size or strength of the mature butterfly, much as what we feed our minds determines our beliefs and mindsets as adults.

Caterpillar diets can control far more than just the size of the adult. They can also affect wing colors, flight durations, mating patterns and warning signals. What the caterpillar feeds itself determines its strength and safety.

It is vitally important to feed our minds optimal data and to monitor what data they feed back to us. We want to bring as much clarity as possible into our quickening chrysalis.

What's wrong with the way we think?

We experience life from within the contents of our minds. What our minds and bodies hold onto form the template or framework from which we develop perspective and from within which we perceive. Think about that for a minute. Your mind sets the stage, picks the props and costumes, and decides what roles you will play in life. How could that be optimal when our minds have been trained and conditioned by the collective limitations of this world?

If you believe you will always be a caterpillar, for example, that is what will happen. Source always says, "yes." I am happy = yes. I am miserable = yes, and so on. Her "yes" sometimes comes in the form of "Not right now," Because She will avoid causing us harm, if possible.

If you think your choices come from something outside of you, think again. We are all conditioned to believe things are a certain way or have to be a certain way. If you did not believe those things, you would act and react differently. You would know to choose from awareness rather than conditioned reactivity.

What does your mind contain that does not serve you? It could be as simple as replacing a consistently negative view of life with a happier one. Changing negative thought patterns to more positive ones is where many of us begin.

The answer to what's wrong with the way we think is that most of our thoughts come from fixed, obsolete systems. We literally need to change our minds. When we begin to pay attention to our thoughts and change them, we benefit immensely.

As humans, we grow up with mind chatter or the recordings in our heads that seem to loop endlessly. We store these thought patterns unconsciously most of the time. We also seed or park them at frequently visited locations. Have you ever driven down your usual road to somewhere and noticed yourself thinking the same thing every time you drive past? You left a thought pattern at that location to guide or inform your journey. Most of the thought patterns you deposit, like breadcrumbs marking your trail, are unnecessary. You have the power to choose to delete them from any location and your internal data storage. Doing so frees energy you will need as you build your chrysalis.

Thought patterns stored in our minds and bodies run on autopilot. Changing the way we think means upgrading or deleting these patterns altogether, replacing them with stillness, or feelings that support our evolution and ascension.

People often say, "Oh, I can do that, that's easy!" then proceed to think in the same old ways and become upset when life doesn't change. Changing the diet you feed your mind is a long-term commitment. Understanding how to practice something doesn't mean you *are* practicing it. Practice makes all the difference.

Preparing your body and mind for enlightened embodiment means allowing your thought patterns, beliefs, and behaviors to shift.

Thought Patterns

A thought pattern forms when we think something over and over again. Synapses wire together in the brain to build a superhighway for these frequently used thoughts, and a rut forms. The least action pathway for our minds is to utilize these well-paved synaptic channels.

Example: "I always ____." Or, "____ always happens." Always and never are clues that a thought pattern or belief system is in place. This kind of thought pattern represents an unconscious choice to use the well-paved superhighway of conditioned response as your least-action pathway. Your brain tells you this is efficient, when most often it is not.

A least-action pathway is not optimal. It is not going with the flow of anything but its architecture. It is a lazy use of the mind's resources.

Pavlov's dogs salivated at the sound of a bell. What are you conditioned to react to in similar ways? Mindfulness begins the process of shifting reactivity into responsibility.

Belief Systems

A belief system is a thought pattern that you argue for. In other words, thoughts that have repeated over and over become a pattern that the mind defends. The mind and emotions make a case for this pattern to stay in place by finding ways to defend it. When the case is good enough, a belief system is formed. The underlying belief is always some variation of "This is good for me. This keeps me safe." That is the voice of the ego, not the truth.

Example: "That is how life is." The implication being that "that" is a fixed condition and cannot be changed. Your education and conditioning will fill in the definition of "that" before you are aware of the thought beginning to form. The way to change this is to go to the source.

Everything is energy. Everything is vibration. Energy and vibration are in constant motion. How then, can anything be the way anything "always is"? Even your logical mind will agree that the premise is unsound. That is the beginning. Recognize the pattern and choose to eliminate or replace it.

Habits of Behavior

A habit of behavior is set in motion as a coping mechanism to reinforce, or provide an antidote to, thought patterns and belief systems.

A reinforcing or antidotal habit of behavior might be to interrupt or talk over someone else's opinion, when the opinion in question threatens your belief systems. It is a conditioned fear response. This behavior tells the person acting it out that they are important, they are right, and the opinion being voiced is irrelevant. There is no need to fear new information or anything that represents the unknown. It is easier to shout it down. Children (and some alleged adults) do this by covering their ears and making noise, or hitting first and asking questions later.

Breaking the habits that waste our energy is vital to awakening. First, we must change how we think, cutting off the energy supply to the habit. Then, we change the habit by replacing it with a higher vibration of information and action.

Listen to the way you speak to yourself and others. Hear your own words. Words have power. They become thoughts. Everything that manifests begins with a thought, powered by a subconscious or unconscious program. Thoughts seed experiences and realities.

Refine and reframe your words. This refines and reframes your thoughts. You can choose what thoughts to think. A way to begin is to reframe the voice you hear in your head and the one that comes out of your mouth. When you hear yourself say something that is the effect of a conditioned response or an old story, stop. Take a breath and correct your words. When you do this, you shift a synaptic pattern in your brain. Synapses that fire together, wire together. How do you choose to be wired?

Example: When you hear yourself say or think "I always…" ask Her, ask your intuition if that is true for you. If you are in the process of awakening you have most likely just encountered a thought pattern, belief system or habit of behavior. In the process of egoic dissolution, it is important to look at all of the ways we self-define by how we think.

We say "I am this, I am not that." This creates our self-identity. Self-identity is the role we play in life. In the process of awakening we do not have the luxury of complacency about who/what we perceive ourselves to be. It is all an illusion. What parts in the life-play serve how we resonate and what parts do not? We begin by releasing the parts that do not serve, then allow Her to upgrade the parts that do serve us.

Use positive reframing. This means changing an intention, for example, from "I want this to stop," to "I now radiate and embody _____." Fill in the blank with what you do want, rather than what you wish would change.

There is a difference between magical thinking, spiritual bypassing, and clarity of mind.

Magical thinking happens when we live in a state of ungrounded wishes and hopes. This is a common trap. We begin to re-train our minds, and fantasy takes over. It's easier. It feels better to wander around Fantasy Island than to do the work of clearing out the garbage in our minds. An example might be "I'll sit here and meditate and wait for what I want to show up." Nothing will happen. She brings us what we are open to receive, by way of the intuitively inspired actions we take. Her remix is, "I will become still, listen for Her guidance, then follow through on what I am given."

Spiritual bypassing is another common affliction among the awakening. This happens when, in the process of re-training the mind, we choose higher octaves of vibration, then ignore where we are still fixed, limited, or being triggered. An example might be "I meditate all the time and none of that stuff bothers me anymore."

This statement is a little suspicious because ignoring triggers is something the lower levels of mind are really good at, and this is a challenging world. Reactivity is what we strive to rise above, and it is a constant work in progress.

Clarity of mind gives us the ability to focus with laser-like intent. It gives our thoughts power. Such clarity is based on truth, not fantasy, not conditioned response.

Mastery of mind is achieved through clarity. Clarity is achieved through the dissolution of the ego and the re-training of the mind. All of the above require a constant commitment to truth.

Her way of mindfulness is in letting go. What clutters the mind with information of little or no value, or concepts that teach us to harm ourselves, can be replaced with Her light. Opening the mind and heart to Her opens us to Infinite possibilities.

She asks that we let Her move through us, that we allow Her to show us new ways to be.

Movement

All movement is born of Stillness. Therefore, it is best to meditate first, then move. Even if you only enter the Stillness for a few minutes prior to being active, your movement will come from a higher octave of energy.

All of nature is in motion. The earth hurtles through space within her orbit, within the orbit of the solar system in the galaxy, and as part of the galaxy's travels through the cosmos. Our cells are in constant motion within our physiology. Everything moves. Everything changes. This is our truest nature.

When we harmonize with what is most natural to us, we can relax into our bodies, ourselves, and our world.

The saying "A body in motion remains in motion. A body at rest remains at rest," is both true and untrue. We are always in motion. Being at rest means being at one with that motion. Stillness seems still because within the Oneness there is no friction. Without friction it is impossible to feel distance or separation.

Why is movement important? The easy answer, that everyone knows, is that physical movement keeps our bodies healthy. It pumps the lymph system. It harmonizes us with nature and cosmic consciousness. A physical practice of movement keeps every level of our energies flowing. It allows us to let obsolete energies move out of our fields.

Moving allows detoxing energies to leave our bodies and minds. It allows us to embody freedom and change. Balanced in our bodies, it is easier for us to ground more light.

There are certain types of movement that help us align with nature. Walking is the simplest and most straight forward. Our bodies were built to walk.

One example of a walking practice is to use a pedometer and take 5,000 steps a day. Any kind of step. Even from your office chair to the hall or bathroom. It is not necessary to power walk, or to walk-run, though that can be more fun or feel more rewarding. As with any practice, consistency is key.

The practice of Chi Walking, founded by Danny Dreyer, revolutionized the intersection of tai chi and walking/running. This is an example of what is possible when we listen to our bodies and what their natural homeostatic (balancing) rhythms can teach us.

Another example is yoga, in its various forms. Pick your favorite and do more than dabble. In terms of physicalizing awareness, or bringing consciousness into your body, some forms of yoga are more helpful than others. Anything too rigid, that forces the body beyond what it wants to do, is counter-productive for consciousness.

The most important thing to remember is to let your body lead. Emily learned to ask her body, "How shall we move today?" As a longtime runner and martial artist, she was used to hard workouts. Anything less felt like a waste of time. The Great Mother reminded her, over and over, that a caterpillar has very different physical needs than a butterfly.

As Emily's body transitioned, it would go through many phases of deep, alchemical morphing, and her movement needs would radically change.
Our bodies need to be grounded through the Earth in ever-changing ways, as we progress from crawling to flight.

In a fitness-addicted culture, it is often difficult to feel what will serve the practice of grounding light and consciousness into the body versus what enslaves us to a stereotypical body image. As you move from who you thought you were to who you might become, you will need to make more conscious choices.

Transformation

We constantly re-invent ourselves. There are countless ways to change our image, our expression, and our voice. With the world in transition, the art of transformation is presenting itself for study in ever increasing ways. Will what we did in the past serve us going forward? How is anyone to know?

This question is addressed again and again in the enlightenment process, as we dissolve the layers of self, going through shamanic death after shamanic death, until we may feel we have no skin left to shed. Then, we find that those were not the biggest changes!

A caterpillar's body dissolves completely within its chrysalis. It liquefies into a gooey substance, made up of bits of DNA. Left within the goo are tiny imaginal disks, similar to embryonic cells. These disks are present within the caterpillar its whole life, but they stop growing at a certain point in the caterpillar's development and only start again when it is time for the caterpillar to morph into a butterfly.

Once the proper time comes, the imaginal disks use nutrients from the digested body of the caterpillar as they form into different parts of the butterfly's body, with different disks forming into different tissues. For instance, there are imaginal disks that will form the legs, antennae, specific organs, etc. of the butterfly. There are even four imaginal disks that form wings. If one of these forming wings is removed, the other three will simply adapt to form bigger wings to compensate for the loss of the one wing. Even caterpillar bodies have cellular intelligence!

The challenge we accept as we choose to awaken is that of the butterfly. Our egos will not want to dissolve into some kind of particularized goo, but they must, even as our physical bodies appear to remain the same.

Our alchemical opus of transformation moves us through our caterpillar stages, into the cocoon, which can then achieve the transparency of a chrysalis, from which we can move into enlightened embodiment.

Shifting From the Heart

Lifting the Veils of Separation

Shifting from the heart integrates your body's and multi-dimensional awareness with your Heartspace. It also begins the lifting of the veils of separation between how you allow yourself to be and how you do not. What exactly does lifting the veils of separation mean? It has to do with both allowing and receiving.

Listening is the gateway to perception. It is an opening into the energies of receptivity. The quality of being receptive has been dismissed, disenfranchised, and denigrated on the planet for approximately 5000 years. Being receptive has come to mean being open to hurt, invasion, and threat. It is the martyr's curse, one of the agreements we all made, as we incarnated into a cycle of martyrdom. It is resisted, at best, and ignored, at worst, within the collective consciousness. We have been programmed and conditioned with resistance to genuine receptivity and the yin power of manifestation for generations. It is time for that to end.

Receptivity is an opening to the Source within all things, not to any specific person, group, place, situation, or thing. It is an immersion in Grace. Open to All That Is, and answers, solutions, and the miraculous flow through you always.

Listening is the beginning of receptivity. A receptive mind is a quiet mind.

When our minds are quiet, we become powerful.

Why Listen, and How?

Any counselor will tell you that the door to better communication is learning to listen. Listening to what another is expressing, leaving personal bias out of the equation, is a gateway to perspective and compassion.

We all admit this is easier said than done. What it takes is practice. Practice at overcoming the conditioning and imprinting we have grown up with that makes us perceive things in a certain way.

Listening to the Divine's voice, whether direct and internal or through the day-to-day expression of someone else, requires that we drop our pre-programmed filters and remain open to the truth.
When anyone wants to be more perceptive, usually to succeed in a particular endeavor, the

first thing they need to learn is to listen to intuition, the voice of the Infinite within.

Listening to your own words, to how you express yourself, is another doorway. What words does your subconscious mind use to communicate? Are these the words Source would use to speak through you?

What voices are my intuition? What voices are those of my patterns? Those who want to learn to listen tell me that they don't know one voice from another. Yes, you do. You will know the truth of these voices by how they feel. The voice of intuition, Source's voice within us comes from a calm, still place. It is peaceful, yet often adamant. It suffers no foolishness, yet is infinitely kind.

The voices of the ego tell us either what we want to hear or what we absolutely don't want to hear, whichever will provoke the reaction that keeps their patterns safe. The Great Mother's voice feels quite different.

The world is noisy. We learn to listen by discerning what feels resonant within our essence and what can be relegated to white noise.

What if I hear the wrong thing? You won't if you are listening from a place of discernment. Her guidance is unmistakable and will not let you make a mistake. Our faceplants come from ignoring Her direction, not from following it.

The Difference Between Hearing and Listening

Listening is a state of receptivity. We enter its domain by opening to the truth. When we listen, we feel for the thread of truth in any information presented. Listening has to do with feeling, in the most real sense of the word. Feeling is not emotion, though emotions point us toward our true feelings. Feeling is seeing and knowing.

Have you ever come across a piece of information or walked into a situation that felt all wrong? Of course you have. Or the opposite. You receive an invitation or contact, and you simply *know* this is right. You are experiencing the intuitive connection that interprets information from Source. It is a part of each of us.

Hearing is simply being present to the noise in our environment. Our auditory senses perceive a vast array of sonic information, far more than our minds process or our brains store. If we hear something and mistake it for intuition, there is a simple test. Does it ring true to your core? Pretend you are a tuning fork and observe how you vibrate. Check the level of dissonance in what you hear.

Selective hearing happens when our filters pre-sort and select, out of the noise surrounding us, what we will notice. Then, our conditioning, patterns, and programs filter what deserves our attention. We don't hear anything else, though it may be present, loud and clear.

When we change our filtering system to that of intuition, selective hearing can work to our advantage. We select *for* the Great Mother's voice instead of all the others.

Selective listening and selective hearing both come from the filters and conditioning we allow to guide our lives. It does not have to be so.

For many of us, as we move into the Heartspace and allow ourselves to clear the ego and dissolve programming, the protective torus isn't quite performing optimally yet. We wonder why more isn't shifting and faster. This is *because we don't allow it*.

The reality construct of your life shows mostly distortion because that's how you have set up your filters and parameters. When we commit to making the unconscious conscious, by definition we are asking to see all of our funhouse mirrors. All of the distortions we hold will show up in the light of day. It can be a bit crazy-making if taken too seriously!

When you look at your reality construct, you're looking at the inside of a mirrored reality representing your ego's inner boundary. You see all the scenes the ego has designed for you to act in, all the roles you play. As your ego becomes transparent, the sections in your funhouse mirror ball become windows, so that you can perceive with clarity.

As you perceive more clearly, you can develop the practice of asking that your remaining mirrors reflect clarity and truth, even if there is still some distortion present. Affirm that your opaque cocoon becomes transparent, like a chrysalis. As you practice, you develop the ability to recognize distortion for what it is and stop taking it personally.

If you can't see distortion for what it is yet, don't worry. Distortion may feel normal to you. For example, when something happens in your life and you get triggered, then somebody else gets triggered, and drama ensues. That's it right there, distortion of truth and clarity. One triggering triggers something else, and so on and so on.

When this happens, use the chrysalis to clean things up immediately. Observe how your reality construct (life experience) mirrors the triggering, then observe the calm when your reactivity has cleared. As you gain mastery of observation, you will notice where there are funhouse or fogged or smudged mirrors in your construct. You will also see your clarity.

When more and more clarity is present, what you will find is that you have a 360-degree hall of windows from within which to perceive life, creation, and light, directly *and without distortion*. Your experiential sphere becomes more flexible, pliable, and translucent, if not transparent.

Some of your windows might have solar shielding. Some might have tinted glass for other reasons. Or perhaps there are still a few funhouse type mirrors kept for hilarious effect. These perceptions, sometimes called phenomena, are a side effect of your inner shifting.

Many of our energies needing transformation are the unconscious archetypal energies we cling to with all our might. This can be especially true if we hold onto particular archetypes that have worked for us in the past and helped us to make quantum leaps. We don't want to let go of those templates. Why would we?

What requires dissolution is the *attachment* we have to a particular archetype, set of circumstances, person, place, or thing. These life attributes can remain happily within the

Great Mother's dry cleaning shop, circling on that massive rack until needed, or we choose to enjoy them.

In this cycle, everything is a fluid crystal palette. To flow with this palette, we need to let even our most cherished fixed forms go. Any place inside that is a fixed form, no matter *how* beneficial, needs to melt. Remember, caterpillars don't fly.

An image that comes to mind is from the film *Terminator Two*, where the Terminator asks to be lowered into a vat of molten steel because that's the only thing that will dissolve its structure and programming. An extreme metaphor, but valuable for our most stubborn programs. The earth is going through a similar dissolution of old forms. Volcanoes are erupting, and magma is on the move. There are changes in wind and water.

These changes activate our bone marrow. The energetic, etheric, and pranic material in our bone marrow is the *same* as the elementals of magma! The same elementals that form new land form our bodies. The essence of our physical structure is changing. Our cellular structures are shifting and becoming more fluid.

The cocooning process, the chrysalis function, does not present a barrier to transmitting, nor is it a barrier to receiving. Our ego would like us to make this mistake. It tells us that if we allow the structure of the chrysalis to remain in place, things we desire cannot come in, and what we don't want will always get in. These are lies the ego tells to protect itself.

Those of us *committed* to the light, committed to the flow of love, don't want to feel resistance. We want to bypass, or ignore it when it shows up. Ignoring or denying our issues is known as spiritual bypassing and puts barriers in the way of awakening. So, forgive yourself when you feel resistance or when doubts arrive. Our egos were constructed to survive and fight to the death. Engaging in this battle does not accomplish anything. Let Her dissolve the resistance. Offer it up, while not buying into it or listening to its voice.

You don't even need to know what the reason for your resistance might be. **All you need is to be willing to release it.** You might think, "Okay, that's been there for whatever reason, I don't care anymore. Take it. Release all of the resistance and defended positions I'm carrying. Release any part of me that says I need this." When the ego-mind dictates to the physical body, it tells the brain that holding onto old synaptic patterns is healthy and beneficial for your survival. The brain then hooks the resistance pattern into your root chakra to engage your physical body in resisting.

The Heartspace provides a flexible, fluid womb of energy, light, and love. The chrysalis provides the transformational space that replaces the physical body as your processing vehicle. The job of transmuting inappropriate or obsolete energies now belongs to the chrysalis.

The chrysalis also needs to replace your current relational field, how you relate to life around you. If you have any fear about hurting someone by shifting how you work with energy or hurting the earth by so doing, those fears need to go into the chrysalis as well. Caveats like these keep you disempowered and help to keep separation in place. She calls them holdouts. We withhold a part of our surrender into Source because a part of our ego thinks it knows better. If this spiritualized ego is surrendered, the chrysalis will transform it.

The chrysalis isn't a wall; it is a transformative space. It performs the highest service there is. **We are walking transformers for ourselves and the world when we take responsibility for clearing whatever shows up in our field.**

Remember the earlier reference to a theater in the round, with you standing in the center? The Reality Construct is your life, the world around you as you currently perceive it. This mode of perception is similar to the scene in the second Matrix movie where Neo walks into the office of the Architect. He sees an infinite number of TV screens with an image of himself on every one. Each screen shows him having a different reaction. This is what is going on in the reflection of your life experience. Which screens, mirrors, or windows are clear? Those are areas with little or no reactivity. When there is no reactivity present, we perceive through the veils, through how we are programmed, into what is real.

Working with these spherical forms begins to give us the point of view of the wave, which is the Divine Mother's point of view. We are all unique particles in the waves – drops in Her sea. As we begin to acquire that point of view, we begin to see what comprises the wave, which pieces we resonate with, and which we do not.

Her Spherical Morphing Wave

A spherical morphing wave is one of the quickest ways to facilitate the clearing process once you have escorted unhelpful energies into your chrysalis' outer layers.

Begin by focusing at the center of your Heartspace. Feel ripples of energy moving outwards as though a stone has dropped into a still pond. Let the ripples become waves, as they travel spherically through your Heartspace. Let your intuition show you how many pulses are needed to refresh your inner sanctuary.

As each ripple touches the boundary of your reality construct, it turns and ripples back to your center. These return ripples don't bring debris. As Spirit's messengers, they bring reflections of truth, clarity, love, and light. Open to the returning waves as much as you can. Let them all the way in, even though your mind may not agree. Your heart does. It needs these waves of rejuvenation and refreshment.

Breathe. Let these energies move through your body, through your stem cells and into the particle level. Release all of your physiology, any conditions, any symptoms, any agreements, vows, or contracts. As this spherical morph takes over, new assemblage points will form, again and again, until your consciousness becomes completely fluid. When will this be complete? The mind won't know when, but the heart will know. Be patient with yourself.

Don't worry. You will be better able to handle the business at hand because the Divine Mother is the ultimate optimizer. She has it handled. She always has and always will.

Daily Practice

You might want a separate journal, or online notes for this practice. Done daily, it takes an average of two weeks for your subconscious mind to get on board and begin to use these guidelines as your new default.

Beginning the Day

Start with relaxing into your Heartspace. Take three conscious breaths, or three sets of three. Why? Manifestation in earth-space-time is a function of threes.

Know that your Heartspace surrounds you as you go about your day. Ask the Divine, "How shall we play today and what shall we create?" Let that intuitive flow guide you through whatever actions you feel called to take. Thank the Divine for giving you guidance all day and helping you to recognize it and follow through.

You can start the day by intending:

I am held in the Heartspace, thank you. Thank you that I will be shown today every bit of intuitive guidance I might need. Thank you that everything needing to transform, will. And thank you that my reality construct is completely, totally and constantly morphing into Divine embodiment. Thank you that I am learning. Thank you that my mind is an ally, fully on board for the ride. Thank you that I will receive all the intuitive guidance I need, all day long, and I am allowing the Heartspace to navigate my day.

{As Emily learned this, she repeated her affirmations of gratitude over and over, throughout the day, whenever she felt challenged.}

Ending the Day

At the end of the day, preferably just before you sleep, check in with yourself. Without score cards or self-judgment, ask yourself these questions. Write your answers down, every day, for about two weeks.

What was my guidance today? What did my intuition tell me? For the information that had action steps, did I follow through?

When you find that you have followed through on every intuitively guided action, even for one day, celebrate and give yourself a treat. This is not a drill! You are teaching your subconscious that you choose to live this way.

Archetypal Allegiances

What exactly is an archetype? An archetype is a piece of what frames our lives. We have many in our unconscious. Archetypes are often larger-than-life identity structures; some are held so deeply within us that we are not aware they are there. We have them in all of the different areas of our lives. The fastest way to begin to observe them is through the children's stories and fairy tales we listened to, growing up. Archetypes are many-aspected characters with roles, costumes, props, and stage sets, playing out in our lives.

They come from our families, our cultures and, very often, from our nationalities, because different national identities have different stories. Consider someone who has always lived in one place, what their attitudes and references might be. Compare that to someone who spends even a small part of their childhood in another location. The one who has lived in differing locales will have vastly different reference points for living than those who have not. It is fascinating to hear the stories children grow up with and observe how many have similar themes and how many are vastly different.

When we clear egoic consciousness, we start with our stories. These stories would be nothing without their defining characters. We tend to be the protagonist or the hero/ine. Some like being the super-villain, and for them, that works. But in truth, we've all been both. We play all the roles. That is the surface level of identity.

Emily was all about strength and intelligence. Wonder Woman, Artemis, Sekhmet, Anne of Green Gables, and Jo March of *Little Women* were some of her role models.

One day, as she sat with the trees, she saw a montage of these role models and the threads they held in common. Added to those from this life were other life images of the Goddess Durga, Tara, and Isis, the High Priestess.

She invoked her Heartspace and its cocooned shelter as she looked into these images. Laughing, she watched her ego imagine that she might have been one of these Goddesses or, at least, the heroine of some of their many adventures. But Emily knew better.

She recognized the threads of bravado, rebel-savior, savior-martyr, healer-savior, and other pieces of the Priestess function. As she listened ever the more deeply, she heard the Great Mother's voice.

"How attached are you to these behaviors? How much does it matter to be a heroine, to be right, to be the one that saves the day? Nothing is wrong with any of the roles you have been playing. My question is, will you continue to let your attachments to these roles limit you?"

Archetypes are held mainly in the unconsciousness, however. Consider the metaphor of an iceberg. The unconscious mind is the part of the berg that's invisible in the sea *below* the waterline. It's much, much bigger than what appears on the surface. This submerged, hidden part of us is doing the navigating in our lives, until we bring it into consciousness. We do that by raising the entire iceberg to the surface. Bit by bit, program by program, carving chunk by chunk, **we make the unconscious, conscious.**

A great way to look at the roles we play, at our conscious archetypes, can be found in Caroline Myss's book, *Sacred Contracts*. Indexed by archetype, with synopses of each, the book is an excellent reference for how we perceive ourselves.

For instance, we might say, "I act out this," or "I always…", "She's the Princess archetype," or

"He's the Structuralist" archetype. It's easy to see the roles others play and, through that observation, observe what our value judgments are about those roles. How do you honestly feel about specific roles?

The voices of archetypal alliance tell you, "I am this, I am not that." These voices show you the identity you have adopted as truth. Other examples might be, "I am an Aries," or "I am this particular energy configuration." These are aspects of you, yes, but they are not your totality. Setting these roles up as fixed parts of your identity limits your ability to shift vibration, awaken, and ascend. Setting them free empowers you.

As we begin to wake-up, we start to reference ourselves as energy configurations more and more. It's more comfortable for the ego to have a frame for the morphing picture we are becoming. There is nothing wrong with this. It is part of the awakening process and is a function of our unconscious. *The issue for those who choose to awaken is that the minute we create a frame, we've created a potential limitation.*

Limits are necessary to have differentiated experiences in reality. Limitations put the brakes on evolving into fluidity.

In this particular incarnation, we have the opportunity to transcend them *all*. There has not been an opportunity like this in any physical world as far as we know. There may have been opportunities like this in other worlds. There are probably parallels going on right now. We don't know *a lot*. She has offered us an unprecedented opportunity, in this world, right now.

We can transcend our archetypes and become fluid.

As Emily meditated on her attachments to the archetypes that showed up, she had a vision. She faced Source across the counter of a dry cleaning shop. A chain of mobile hangars wound behind the counter, obscured only a little by the intense light of Presence. Every costume for every role Emily had ever played or aspired to play hung on that mobile rack, organized just so.

As Emily gazed in wonder, she felt a Hand take hers. Firmly but gently, she was turned 180 degrees to face away from the infinite array of attire. Beams of light shone through her in prismatic spectrum, each illuminating a set of circumstances. In each of those circumstances, Emily, the lead character, was clothed in precisely the garments, gifts, talents, abilities, and attributes required to complete the task.

It was all perfectly orchestrated and arranged. She knew, with every part of her, that she must learn from her chosen archetypal allegiances and then surrender them. Each was a gift of learning about embodiment. The infinite array of choices would be there for her, always, if only she would show up, in the moment, and let Source choose.

Emily's raptured sigh opened her heart. Compassion for the roles she was playing flowed through her, as she laughed, and put the dreams of childish awareness behind her.

"I could be anything, anyone, and it would be all right," she whispered to the Great Mother.

With this revelation, Emily began her journey through the egoic core, dismantling bits of it and discarding others until she began to glow.

How to Release Archetypal Allegiance

We all have our favorites. These chosen roles and identities hang close to the front of Source's mobile rack for us. The trick is in knowing that how we show up is yet another scripted or unscripted character, and surrendering the play and our part in it to Source for optimization.

Begin by invoking your Heartspace by making it conscious. Include your cocoon or chrysalis in your visualization. Take a moment to notice whether the buffering layer is showing up more opaquely, like a cocoon, or transparently like a chrysalis. Your level of opacity or transparency is useful information. It gives you an indication of how much work there is yet to do in this area. You will notice, as you use Her tools, the various qualities, and densities of your protective orb.

Once you are resting in your Heartspace, with an activated Chrysalis, you are ready to begin.

What roles have you been playing today? What shows up first are probably the functional archetypes that get you through your day. Let these friends rest in the Heartspace, asking that anything that could use an upgrade is moved into the cocoon layer and shifted. These withholds include thought patterns, belief systems, and some habits of behavior associated with the roles you play.

As your obsolete patterns begin to clear, you may notice your protective orb looks less like a cocoon and more transparent, like a chrysalis. Where you let go of attachment to being seen in a certain way, is where Her light gets in.

Maybe you're good at surrender, maybe not. Emily had *views* on the subject. Her answer to surrender was, "Never!" She had not yet understood.

The voice of the Great Mother echoed in her ears.

"Surrender is not giving up or giving over to anyone or anything outside of you. It is letting Me in and letting the part of Me that you are, take over."

If you think you can't live without an archetype, it's got you. That part of your ego has you handcuffed. It isn't that you don't want that particular archetype in your closet, or your energetic repertoire. You do. You chose those skills, that wisdom, those talents, those abilities. What you don't want is for your chosen qualities to become limitations. Every time we allow an archetype to define us, we restrict Source's ability to play through us in whatever way is optimal in the moment.

The more you awaken, the more you will want Source to play through you as the Divine instrument that you are.

Emily so wanted the Divine symphony to play through her she was willing to give up everything else. At the moment she realized this, she understood the lesson of the butterfly.

"If you want to fly, you have to give up being a caterpillar."

Allowing archetypes to play through us as Spirit wills is a fluid way of living. When we identify, when we put that costume on and nail it down, we limit our awakening, no matter how functional a given identity may seem.

You need to consider how the content of an archetype benefits you versus how its context might be limiting you. Let that digest for a bit. Rest in your Heartspace and let its threshing process sort you out.

Your ego may tell you it needs a specific mask or costume to function. We all wear our various masks as we learn to perform in the world. There is no wrong in that. What to look for is when your ego says you have to function from within a particular box. A belief like that creates limitations.

Spend as long as you like in the Heartspace and cocoon/chrysalis. The more you use this clearing process, the faster it happens.

You may find that pieces of information from other chapters find their way into your contemplation. Let them come in and release.

Emily noticed that her biggest holdouts were where she was still insisting on being conditional. Her ego was setting conditions on Source. She felt outraged at the disenfranchisement of women. She wanted to fight.

It took years for the Great Mother's counsel to get through.

"*Do you think you can defend what is precious better than I can?*"

Emily's answer shocked and shamed her. "But you don't help! You don't save them! Atrocities happen every day! Why is this still happening? Why does it happen *every single day*?!"

The Great Mother's answer was patient and kind. "As long as one Spirit chooses to learn from pain and suffering or the illusion of powerlessness, I will support it."

Somewhere, inside Her voice, Emily heard the truth. As hard as it was to face, she understood that if she were willing to let go of every last fiber of accusation and aggression in herself, life would cease to mirror it to her. It didn't mean the world would change. It didn't mean those bad things would stop happening to good people. It meant that Emily's point of view had to change.

Emily wept. The task felt impossible.

"You have forever," the Great Mother soothed. "Or, you can let me be the doer and do the doing. You can let me take care of you. The choice is yours."

As you spin your cocoon and begin to dissolve, remember the Great Mother is your ally. How could She not be? She is yourself.

Working with your archetypes is a step in moving into radical self-honesty. What are you holding onto, and where have you let Her take over? You can choose again at any moment. Send your old choices into the cocoon/chrysalis and watch your field lighten up.

You may want to look at the overarching archetypal forms of this world, like the various dimensions. You are a multi-dimensional being. Your essence does not and cannot live in only one dimension.

The Jungian archetypes of the tyrant, victim, rebel, savior, and the Goddess archetypes of the maiden, mother, {queen}, and crone, cannot be transcended separately. They are part of your reality construct and the framing of the global collective. You can deconstruct pieces of these larger morphogenetic fields as they show up for dissolution, but their grand release will come with awakening. These archetypes are mostly responsible for limiting your ability to perceive multi-dimensionally. They are all part of the veils, the limits that define your world experience. It is worth the effort to deconstruct them.

The good news is that you can always choose a broader perspective.

As you delve into your archetypal allegiances, you may want to investigate your biological inheritance, nationality, astrological blueprint, and any other templates you have ignored or taken for granted. What you find may surprise you. Most of us ignore our most obvious templates and archetypal forms. We believe that's the way things are.

Nothing is the way anything is. We see what we have been taught to recognize. Infants see waves of light and color. Persistent shapes and vibrations are labeled and given words to describe them. And so the world is learned through labels. Nothing wrong with that. But unless we make quantum leaps in perception, our post-embodiment experiences will be much the same as what we experience now. Our alignments, allegiances, and agreements persist.

Working at this level, we can ask what agreements hold our archetypes in place. We don't need to carry them around anymore. Gaia is entirely fluid, whether it looks like it or not. The world is becoming something so new that we can simply look forward to the transformative experience.

As you dissolve your attachments to the archetypes of your life, you see the agreements holding them in place, any rules you agreed to, to protect them, and all other circumstances and plotlines based upon them. As your cocoon shifts into chrysalis-like transparency, it becomes translucent shifting energy. Your protective space begins to reflect the fluid beauty radiating from your heart.

Your reality construct will look less and less like a disco ball turned inward, mirroring your every pattern and program, and more like a sphere of windows whose clarity and reflections show you the truth. Through the windows of clarity, you can perceive life directly, in wonder. What Is enlightenment, if not a direct perception of the miracle of life, without mental limitations?

The practical application of archetypal release and egoic dissolution is in the freedom it brings, to perceive, and to flow with Source as the world changes.

As you rest in your Heartspace, you can use gratitude to ease your way. "Thank you for the gift of this release. Thank you for the optimization. I choose to trust. I am willing to trust. I choose to let my attachments to these old identities release."

As Emily said these words, out loud to Source, she felt a great shifting begin. She knew she was no longer willing to make these attachments real. She aligned herself with whatever optimized experience of reality the Great Mother offered. With that, she agreed not to keep creating an archetype called "The Real World."

Once we relinquish our egoic hold on how we want things to be, we don't know what to do. We can feel like we've lost our most trusted counselor. We don't know what will help, or what will work for us. Source knows. And we are part of Her.

Emily heard the words loud and clear. *"Who do you think you are? Are you the ego?"*

An archetype is all about who your ego has chosen to be. Some roles, costumes, and props are fun to play with and enjoy. We can love them, sometimes leave them, sometimes live with them. Most often, we learn from them and move past them. Once we know that they are all Source playing through us, we are free to enjoy the playing and let Her guide the script.

You don't need a limiting identity, no matter how cool it might be. You would soon tire of even your favorite costume if you wore it every day!

Being a conscious facet of the Oneness is what we incarnated here to learn and to become.

Within that Oneness, all archetypes exist. All choices and agreements are honored.

Why does Oneness seem so difficult? We get our agreements in a bunch.

Shifting Genetic Patterns
~
Using epigenetics to your advantage

One of the most useful new sciences, from the point of view of cellular transformation, is epigenetics. This science reports what the avatars of consciousness have known all along. Our genes are not fixed. Our genetics are influenced by environment, especially the environment created by thoughts, emotions, subconscious and unconscious programs, and their vibrations.

As we delve into genetic readout, we're diving into our DNA. You are not obligated to become conscious of the deep genetic programming you carry, but if you want to transcend physical limitations, you must. Most of these patterns came standard on the vehicle. You have a body, and it carries patterns and programs. Some of these you may love or enjoy, others you put up with, struggle with, or create ways to manage.

It can help to remember that what you are after is a state-shift, a morphing into something new. The goal of genetic clearing is to affect the readout, the interpretive dance of your genetic programs so that you can move into a more expanded state of being.

We choose our parents and our bloodlines to learn from, transcend, and ultimately transform.

But/and a lot of other things come with our physical packages! For example, some companies still automatically put a cigarette lighter in a car. You didn't want it, but it was a standard feature unless you specifically requested the digital port instead. It's the same with our bodies.

Inception

Your physical body's inception point was your choice to incarnate, to experience this or any other lifetime. You chose your talents and abilities, lessons, learning modalities, and options for parentage, genetics, and conditioning that would come closest to meeting your design specifications. Then you, as the fractal of the Universe that you are, chose your entry date/time and set things in motion.

The image of the egg was laid, baby caterpillar fully formed as an intention.

Conception

Your body's conception point was, obviously, a conjoining of egg and sperm, including the traits, characteristics, and patterns carried by those cells.

Our genetic blueprint contains two sets of genes, one paternal, one maternal. Even in utero, environmental factors determine which set of genes will express its characteristics through us. Science used to believe this expression is fated, that it controls us. The enlightenment process, and now epigenetics, proves otherwise.

Our auric field, mirrored by our neural networks, is the environment that shapes our experience. Mind {the filtered and interpreted perception of reality} and brain {the physical perceiver of experience} working together give us our impression of life. Science is only beginning to teach this, while wisdom traditions have shared it for thousands of years.

Spirit merges and bonds with the fetus in utero. During that process, and before, the embryo grows in a physically sterile environment. It is the birth process that exposes the infant body to microbes, through the birth canal and the mother's skin. In utero, the fetus is easily imprinted by the external environment through the placenta and the mother's thoughts and feelings.

Once our Spirit integrates into physical form, the fine print in our incarnational contract tells us to forget everything that happened during the design phase! Our infant body holds onto genetic and environmental patterns without conscious awareness of doing so. The forgetting process stores those designs in our unconscious. When we choose to awaken, we choose to make what is unconscious, conscious. So, these patterns must come to light.

Some patterns keep our bodies happy and healthy. Some of these are the genetic markers that our bodies need to maintain structural integrity. Our physiology is well aware of what it requires and what is decoration. Some patterns present obstacles to the experience of Oneness, enlightenment, and ascension. Even structural patterns can morph and change, though we've been taught, and our bodies have been programmed to believe, that they can't.

The body is brilliant and knows how to keep what it needs and let go of the rest. Anything we've been told, like, 'You have a genetic marker for this disease,' is not necessarily true. We are capable of making thousands of copies of our genetic material, each determined by environment, and defining our experience of it. If we believe and internalize what we have been told, our bodies will make it so. We can also say "no" – any of that information, those fear-based beliefs, can go into the chrysalis where they can shift and change.

New signals form new cellular intelligence. Our bodies are always grateful. It is our choice which patterns to keep and which to surrender. Or, we can learn to let Source choose through us.

Imprints and Implants

Imprinting is a conditioned response. We have cellular genetic imprints, which are energetic and layer onto our DNA. Our bodies are usually programmed to believe that these imprints are permanent, that they have to hold onto these until they die.

Our bodies acquire imprints from the moment of conception. The moment the sperm and the egg meet, the imprinting process begins. Our bodies internalize thought patterns, emotions, and perceptions about life from our mother's body and the environment.

Shifting Genetic Patterns

"The striking transformation of a caterpillar into a colorful, winged butterfly has captivated scientists for years. The metamorphosis involves the breakdown of most of the caterpillar's tissues before reassembling to form a butterfly. It, therefore, seems unlikely that butterflies or moths would remember experiences from their caterpillar days. However, scientists have now established that not only can a moth retain memories formed while it was a caterpillar, but that experiences gained during these early stages can have drastic impacts on adult life." http://www.todayifoundout.com/index.php/2011/10/caterpillars-melt-almost-completely-before-growing-into-butterflies-in-the-chrysalis/

So, too, human infants retain memories from their gestation and what some call past-life experiences. The brainstem, the area of the medulla oblongata, holds a set of conditions for your body's physical survival, formed from your DNA and in utero imprinting.

Based on this information and your experiences within the first eight hours or so after your umbilical cord is cut, the brainstem creates a foundational baseline for survival. This might work for creatures in the wild, but it rarely serves a being in a human body in this world.

This baseline in the brainstem sends signals to the limbic or emotional brain, according to the parameters of your birth experience. The limbic brain then sends a corresponding bio-chemical drip to the brainstem and adrenals, causing your body to react to the brain's perceived threat to your survival. In spiritual practice, the brainstem is sometimes called the Reptilian brain. Its sole purpose is to keep the physical body from harm. We need this part of our brain to fulfill its primary function. But we need it to do so from a more informed, responsive place.

When we shift the heart, we also shift the brain. In the early stages of embryonic development, the organs of brain and heart form as one. As the fetus develops and uncurls, the brain and heart differentiate into their respective functional organs, retaining the instinctual coding for working in harmony.

As you move into releasing obsolete genetic resonance, you can let the brainstem and the heart muscle release any shared programming that your Spirit knows no longer serves you. Allow the Reptilian brain to be re-educated, and to upgrade its baseline software. A butterfly has very different survival needs than a caterpillar!

Implanting is slightly different than imprinting, though their data is stored in much the same way. An implant happens when someone or something installs something in us, much like we microchip our companion animals. Most implants occur from birth to four - seven years of age or even in utero. They usually take the form of an idea, rule, or some other kind of energy structure. Unlike an imprint, we tend to be more conscious of our implants, even though we like to feel victimized by the process. Usually, implanting is done by people close to us, our parents or caregivers, teachers, etc. One example of implanting might be tribal loyalties and beliefs.

Implants act like rudders, affecting how we navigate the world. So releasing implanting removes the single CD player with its pre-programmed content that we were born with. We choose to upgrade because we want more evolved features.

Bloodlines

We sometimes choose our parents because of the bloodlines they carry. Certain gifts, talents, and abilities are most readily available when acquired genetically.

To start your upgrade, let your body be aware that these factors are in play. Offer into the chrysalis *any* bloodline patterns, whether you are conscious of them or not, that no longer serve you. Some of them may never have. Some of them are national, cultural, racial, tribal, archetypal, or samskaric, meaning they carry over from other lives.

We sometimes bring our past life patterns in through our bloodlines and our DNA. It's an efficient method of installing a program we want to work with, in any lifetime. We might intend, "Oh, I've got this thing I still want to work on in another life, so I'm going to choose a family with that pattern. It will become encoded into my cellular structures, and so I will have no choice." *That was then*. But now, we've reached a point in consciousness where this type of mechanism is no longer needed to help us evolve.

Bloodline programs have to do with your family tree. You have ovum genes, imprints, and implants from your mother's side, and seminal genes, imprints, and implants from your father's. Many of these patterns go back multiple generations. When you begin to allow these patterns to upgrade, release, and run at optimal, you need to set the intention that what will not serve you *now* dissolves back to when it was *first* put in place. This means releasing a flow back to the inception of your bloodline pattern, however many generations ago that may have been.

Let the intended release cascade through all generations, through your own body, and into the future so that any children you might have or want to have, will not automatically carry this programming forward.

Your ancestors will thank you! When we ask the Great Mother for this type of release, we make the clearing available to anyone carrying a piece of our bloodlines. We can intend that they receive the benefit of this release whenever they are ready and willing to accept it.

Optimizing the family tree works for blood family, any type of immediate family, extended and adopted family as well. This includes our spiritual and chosen family groups. We all carry genes from the original thirteen grandmothers. Optimizing your bloodline patterns can assist others you may never meet!

If you're ready to release at the genetic level, it helps to work with an energy healer who understands these principles, but it is not always necessary. Using the Heartspace, Chrysalis and the mirroring of your Reality Construct, you can help your body to let go and transform. The Great Mother is always with us, to assist us in our transformation.

Symptom Causing Patterns

Symptom causing patterns are the most active patterns running in our subconscious minds. They determine most of our actions and habits of behavior. These internal lines of code were inherited or set in place between our gestation in utero and four to seven years of age. Most of these we take for granted, as part of us, or "how things are."

Imagine tendrils of dandelion root, crawling under anything they can, including pavement and the rest of the garden. These roots invade as much territory as possible, propagating as they go, much like a virus. That's what symptom-causing patterns do. They wreak the most havoc in our physical bodies and lives by affecting as many systems as possible.

Symptom-causing patterns are *not* the big girders of consciousness that hold our framework of life together, but they make us believe that without them, we will die. It's one of their best failsafes. These agreements are an artificial intelligence system, finding anything physical, emotional, mental, or spiritual to empower themselves.

Did you know that you can have a runny nose, or a garden hose or pipe can break, and these events can come from the same pattern? In the same way, a stubbed toe or a fender bender can have the same source. Symptom-causing patterns will use *anything* because **they are programmed to protect their survival.**

Let's compare these patterns with the mechanics of disease. What are the main causes of disease? The three T's: trauma, toxins, and thoughts. Each of these presents a particular type of stressor to our systems.

Trauma represents physical stress. Toxins are chemical stress. Thoughts are energetic stress. Everything begins with energy. Everything in the physical world begins with a thought. Releasing symptom-causing patterns begins by examining what we allow ourselves to think.

The more conscious we become of our diet of thought, the healthier we can become.

Memories of trauma, conscious or unconscious, create traumatic stress. According to Wikipedia, "About 8 million adults experience PTSD during a given year." Statistics based on the American population. (Dis)tress is a precursor for disease.

Symptom causing patterns always have hooks into the brain stem and the root chakra in order to take advantage of the HPA axis. {hypothalamus, pituitary, adrenal} They can drag us into fight, flight, or freeze by triggering the fear response. They tend to grab onto any genetic weakness, especially fear-based patterns wired into our DNA. In this way, our patterns use the stress response to propagate their agendas and keep themselves running.

A pattern has one or more triggers, a set of symptoms, and a rule that holds it all in place. That's the general *structure* of these programs. What you want to accomplish in releasing them is to have the subconscious mind and the brain stem recognize an available upgrade that ensures survival better than what it is running now.

These programs do not have any more power over you than you give them. You can choose to ignore them, develop workarounds for them, or go for the upgrade. Those like Emily will always choose the red pill, "I'm going for the taproot. I'm going to allow Source to dissolve the root cause of this pattern, and then the rest of the programs can wither and dissolve."

Working with Symptom Causing Patterns

Working on releasing symptom-causing patterns at an energetic level, we get to understand how the mind keeps them in play. Consciously, we wouldn't choose to have accidents or be in pain or contract a disease. But unconsciously? We have agreements and patterns that cause the events we call illness and accidents.

When we have persisting symptoms, it is because they are programmed into us to keep us safe. Their agenda is to keep our physical body and spiritual essence alive. Our bodies know this, in the way that a caterpillar instinctively avoids certain toxic substances.

Most of these symptomatic protections don't make sense to our logical, adult minds. Many of them developed in utero and are, therefore, pre-verbal. They simply act out until we dissolve what triggers them.

When we're doing self-inquiry, it's helpful to feel into the energy, the vibration of the physical symptoms or situation presenting itself. We need to be able to see what is primary and causal and why. Past-life memories or karmas may affect these patterns, but they are not the primary focus when we choose to release what is impacting our lives. The thing to focus on is what is going on in *this* body, in *this life.* It is here that we are experiencing the symptoms.

Starting with the obvious helps. Was or is there trauma involved? Toxicity? What thoughts have we been thinking? This kind of observation shows us our belief systems about the situation. We are so conditioned to believe things happen in a certain way, for certain reasons, but do they?

Let's talk a little more about the structures of these patterns. How they *sit* in our bodies, our physical, emotional, and mental bodies; how they play off one another to keep running, even when we're tired of them, have had enough and want them to be gone, especially if they're uncomfortable. "I'm sick of this!" is a significant clue. When we tell our bodies we are sick, they tend to comply.

Though we may be experiencing physical symptoms, t*hese are spiritual and emotional pathologies*. It's all energy. These patterns are ways of describing different vibrations that have the same source. If a symptomatic pattern persists, some part of you feels that your *survival,* at some level, depends on having it there.

The first thing you want to do is to *choose* to have compassion for whatever part of you feels threatened. Try telling yourself, "I'm willing to *accept* what feels that this is necessary. I don't like it, but I'm willing to accept it." Compassion is a cool emotion. Its essence is calm and even. Start there. It's more challenging than it might seem.

Then take a look. You're offering compassion, not sympathy, to the part of yourself that's holding on. Whether it's a vibration, whether it's a persona that you can name, whatever it might be, address it directly. "What is the benefit of this?"

It helps to choose to *accept* the answer no matter what it is because you're probably not going to like it. Especially if you're in pain. If the symptom involves *significant* discomfort of some kind, whether physical or emotional, you want it gone and want it gone yesterday. It's perfectly reasonable to feel that way. But, there's an energy in you that says your survival depends on this.

Let that go from the brain stem, your stem cells, your core. Intention counts more than what you think. Escort your resistance gently into your releasing buffer. Remind it that you're shifting. You're upgrading your system, so it is more functional and has a cleaner energy burn.

You can tell any resistant part of yourself that allowing it to transform reduces your inner toxic imprint. Use whatever verbiage works to calm your brain, adrenals, and body chemistry. There is no threat, no tiger in the room. You will not lose vital energy. This pattern will transform into something that works more efficiently. The body will listen if you are patient and treat it with respect.

Take a moment or two, now, to listen to any pattern that might be surfacing. What is the benefit? What is its reason to live? We know it's a survival pattern, that's a given. Ask what benefit you have *refused* to listen to or that you don't want to hear. There is something there, or you wouldn't be having the symptoms.

You may see and feel many layers, and you may get a "piss off" response from your body because you haven't paid attention to it in the past. Don't get upset. A childish pattern is acting out within you. Be patient and listen. Ask the pattern what it needs you to hear. Ask how it is assisting you. Then, listen. The first step is getting the pattern's voice to answer you. If it doesn't want to yet, be patient. It will.

The next step is to ask where, in the physical body, the pattern has its roots. If you are having physical symptoms, you may think this is obvious. It may be, but there is typically a deeper current running far beneath the symptoms. Where does the pattern have a hook into you? What if the symptom is showing up in one place, and the *source* of it is elsewhere? What do your feelings tell you?

Pieces of the pattern might be what you find first. Locate whatever you can, wherever you find a chink in the armor. You might find the whole pattern, you might find its trigger first, and you will notice the symptoms because you're dealing with them.

There is always an underlying agreement, a conditioned response, locking our patterns in place. It could be anything that dictates how the pattern functions. It's like a line of code in a software program. You can feel the inner agreement wherever its vibration is the strongest. We observe your reality construct as part of this excavation, because it is an extension of your physical body, and holds the pattern's reflections.

It can help to remember that pain, discomfort, constriction, and limitation of any kind are conditioned responses based on circumstances.

The structure of these patterns is based on a rule or contract. It has a trigger and symptoms. They are the perceptual states that involve all of your bodies; physical, emotional, mental, spiritual, and psychic.

***

The fluffy black lamb was almost big enough for Emily to ride. She hugged it, loving the warmth and security of her new friend. What a terrific birthday surprise! Grandma had certainly gotten it right! And then, when her grandparents left to go home, it happened.

"I'm giving black lambie away," her mother said. "You know you can't have black things. Black has negative energy."

What? thought Emily, terribly confused. She was still under the impression that if she contradicted her mother, lightning would surely strike her dead. But this didn't make sense. Emily knew she wasn't supposed to wear black. That seemed silly, but she wasn't old enough to choose her clothes anyway.
Black lambie disappeared, and Emily forgot all about her. Or so she thought.

Later, as Emily dissected her childhood programming, she remembered. The core misperception of "everything I love will be lost, stolen, denied, leave me or die," dredged up black lambie first and foremost. Wow! Emily could hardly believe her body had kept that memory tucked away. What else did her body remember as a traumatic loss, that her mind had long forgotten?

Her body chimed right in with "I'm not allowed to have what I want. I can have small things, inconsequential things, but not what I truly want or how I choose to live." Was this to keep her on track, or to limit her awareness? Could her body tell the difference?

As Emily awakened, more and more memories surfaced. More belief systems tracked back to the core perception of not deserving or not being allowed to have what she loved. None of it made sense, except that it did. As her body released the records and memories, the trauma imprints and triggers, she felt it begin to panic.

As her patterns began to release, Emily felt great. Then, after a while, she would feel the grip of fear, and more symptoms would show up. A friend would betray her. Just when she moved into what she thought was a dream home or situation, things would fall apart. She would either be left holding the bag or ripped off and alone. Sometimes both. As these scenarios happened, again and again, Emily realized that though she had released pieces of the pattern, it must still be running. How? What would make it stop?

Emily's pattern is typical of how we set ourselves up. Even though this symptom-causing pattern had been released, for the most part, there was an underlying system of some kind keeping a larger version of it in place.

A *lot* of our patterns form in utero when our mothers were pregnant with us. That's where we get our mother's programming *and* our grandmother's.

As infants, we had no reference point for this world nor the tools to identify fact from fiction, so we soaked up information by osmosis. There is nowhere to assign blame here. Infants learn by copying. Our bodies learn, "this is the way things work."

Most agreements imprint deeply, in our first *day* of life. The reptilian brain, or the brain stem, closes its programming input window at about eight hours after the umbilical cord is cut. The brain stem code has already decided which vibrations are good for our physical survival and which ones are potential threats. The limbic brain, the emotional brain, which is very developed when we're born, really ought to be providing information to the reptilian brain to keep it learning. That's how an open, fully functioning, and balanced brain is supposed to work. But most of us have what we call stress baselines.

In Emily's case, she had a stress baseline about deserving, having her desires supported. It held a massive block of denial activated whenever Emily began to create or receive the life she chose. This unconscious program dictated the terms of her life.

***

We all have unconsciously held patterns that function in this way. They get more and more wily and subtle as we uncover them. None of us needs to spend another big chunk of this incarnation uncovering layer after layer of these patterns. We can no longer afford the time to repair the damage. Better to locate and eliminate the cause.

To synthesize all of this, and release whatever it brought up, drop back into your Heartspace and let yourself be held. Allow the triple container to form around you. We came into this life to learn from and transcend our programming. Its time has come.

It's time to call everything out and send all of your findings into the chrysalis to be transformed. Time to let these limitations go.

You don't need to know what you don't know. That's your mind getting in the way. Our minds are programmed to think they have to *know* before we can move forward. The body has an innate knowing, intuition, and instinct that can be trusted. The Great Mother, the Source of us all, is everything. Her knowing can flow through us once we eliminate the obstacles to Her path.

Reassure your mind. You won't lose it. It will remember how to function in your daily life. Your mind will be functional and competent, more so in fact, without these patterns. The Divine is within every cell, every atom, and every molecule of your body.

The frequencies for discovery and release are simple. Breathe deeply into your heart center and release whatever has happened in your day so far. Let go of whatever is yet to come. Breathe and release.

Breathe naturally and normally, using every part of your lungs. Let your lungs and diaphragm relax as you expand your Heartspace. Allow its energy to expand spherically, letting your Heartspace *contain* your physical, emotional, and mental bodies, with a particular focus on the subconscious mind.

With each breath, expand your Heartspace until you feel held inside it. Let the Divine hold you. Let Her infinite field support you. Allow yourself to be wholly enfolded, no matter what you think you've done in this or any other life, no matter what anyone else thinks you've done in this or any other life, and no matter what programs surface. Your sacred space is not about worthiness or deserving. The Heartspace is Her love in action.

Allow all dissonance, whatever it might be, to move out through the Heartspace boundary into your chrysalis. This is a one-way boundary. Anything can move out, but the only things permitted to enter your Heartspace are truly supportive energies.

From this point forward, you can practice the truth that all energies which no longer resonate with your authentic essence and intentions can move directly into the chrysalis. The movement happens instantaneously and in real-time.

When you feel something uncomfortable, you're triggered, or a known pattern kicks in, use your intent to direct those energies into the chrysalis. Remember, the chrysalis surrounds the Heartspace like a buffer zone and can siphon non-resonant energy from it for transformation.

We came into this incarnation knowing we would need enough power, enough presence, and enough consciousness for this transitional time. We need all of our energies, even though they may be tied up in weird knots, causing us discomfort. So we send these energies into the chrysalis, asking Source to untie them and transform them into whatever *will* be useful for us. We don't need to know what needs to happen. She does. Our field energies will shift into whatever form we require.

Conception Point Release Meditation

The following is an edited transcription of my Conception Point Release guided meditation. The process can be used any time you feel the need for a systematic re-set.

You can record it and play it back to yourself, hearing your own voice guide you, {or translate it into your native tongue} or you are welcome to purchase the recording from my website.

Put yourself into a meditative state. Quiet your mind. Be aware of the Heartspace surrounding you, the chrysalis permeating and enfolding it, and allow Source to guide your transformation. Anything you no longer need is being drawn into the chrysalis enclosure to be transmuted into ascension.

Take three deep relaxed breaths, intending that each cell in your body is super-oxygenated. Then, take three more breaths, intending that each of your cells is infused with life force {chi, ki, or prana}. Take three more breaths, breathing starlight into every cell of your body, especially into your bone marrow. Let your blood circulate the light within you.

Let Source take you on a journey, through this lifetime. You're going to do a fast backward, not a rewind. Rewind implies that the same energies and experiences come back through the body. This is not that. This is a fast backward through your current adult life, your young adult life, adolescence, childhood, and then your toddler years and infancy.

Let yourself be drawn back, observing from your current state of awareness. Remember, you're being drawn back by the Divine Mother, so it's very safe. Nothing is going to re-imprint. Let your body re-experience the birth experience, back through the third trimester of pregnancy, the second trimester, and the first. Now, back to your conception point and to just before that, before the egg and sperm joined.

Let your physical body remember your original design; remind it that you have two blueprints for this life. The first was your caterpillar template. The next is when you reconfigure, resurrect and fly. It's time for the new one to come fully into the body. It's time for you to be the embodiment that was part of this plan,

Conception Point Release Meditation

where you are in alignment with Divine agenda. Go back to this point and let yourself feel your authentic vibrational frequency. Before conception. Before you donned the suit. Whatever images or feelings you receive as you observe are perfect because they're yours.

Now, pay attention. Let your body ground in Her Heartspace. Listen to Her precise instruction for your physical body, emotional body, brain, and deep levels of mind, as you move forward. This is an energetic rebirth. You will not pick up imprints, implants, or genetic programs that no longer serve you as you move through your lifetime.

Feel your awareness begin to move into your conception point. It's an awareness of your second blueprint and of who you are. Anything that your conception imprinted the first time is blowing away. Anything programmed in your first and second trimesters of gestation is now shifting. Let your adult body release it and then move into the third trimester. Let your heart and brain gently release inherited imprints, implants, and anything else you no longer need. If anything feels like a sticking point, make a mental note of it and move on.

Next, move into your birth experience. Let Her spherical morphing waves wash away anything that no longer serves you as you move this vibrational expression of who you are into infancy and then the toddler years. Your body realizes, "Oh, there's this walking thing, we do vertical here. There's a different way to relate to the world than crawling around on the ground." And then move into childhood, the development of the neocortex, the thinking brain, and release anything that it doesn't need – belief systems, thought patterns and habits of behavior. Now you're into the tween years, then the teenage years, letting the balance of the hormonal patterns mature.

Move into young adulthood, into your adult process and let this star being that you are sweep forward until it comes fully into your current adult body. Let it into every cell, molecule, atom, and into your sub-cellular structure. Let it into the myelin sheathing of the nerves, the neural nets, the aura, the bones, the bone marrow, the cartilage, the RNA, DNA, and all of your receptors, channels, and transmitters. Let this essence completely inform them all.

Let any old patterns be forgotten. Your brain will have imprinted the memories, but let them no longer be real. Give your body every opportunity to release them as part of your reality. This process will unfold over what we call time.

Your body awareness will change, moving things that have been taken for granted out of the *way. The release may uncover some new or long-forgotten things, too.*

Now, take three more deep breaths, preferably of starlight, and bring full awareness into a new physical experience.

Shifting Core Agendas

Some say you can't change who you are. With what you've read here so far, I hope you're beginning to understand how flexible identity is, both on the surface and at the core. One of the lessons available in this incarnation is that of total state-shift, enlightenment or ascension.

When you begin working with your core patterns, other patterns will kick up to distract you. These patterns pop up to defend themselves and what lies beneath them. When you feel you've touched on a core program, something else will kick in to grab your attention. "Pay attention to this, answer this email or text," or someone will phone you or the inner voice will set up something else you need to do. What you need to know is that *this is a distraction*. It is not a block. It doesn't even qualify as resistance, although it functions that way. The symptoms or events you're experiencing are your ego fighting for its existence.

Shifting Core Agendas

Your core essence is the divine energy and "star stuff" that you are. Your essence is part of the Divine Mother, part of Source. Why would you want to shift that?

In its unprogrammed state, your core essence does not need to change at all and changes all the time. The programmed pieces of your energy field become ego-driven energies. These implants and imprints become part of what you believe you are. You may be happy with that. You may feel you only want to transform pieces of your body, life, or mind. There is nothing wrong with that.

The choice to live a Source-directed life means these energies must shift into closer alignment with that Source.

The most deeply imprinted energies, those we take on in utero or as young children, become core imprints. Our core imprints form a baseline or template for our ego.

Even core imprints can dissolve, using the chrysalis. The more distractions show up for you, the closer you may be to dissolving your core imprints. If you've been practicing, you've become quite familiar with the chrysalis by now. You know what to do when you notice any unhelpful distractions masquerading as support. Offer them all up and send them into the chrysalis right away. These are the parts of *ourselves* that are trying to distract us from morphing. They don't do this to be pesky and irritating. It may feel that way, but these distractions are being called forth by a core imprint to prevent release. The brainstem doesn't think it's safe to shift a program etched on the core. It needs better information.

First, acknowledge the distracting energies. You will get better results from accepting their presence than from telling them off. Thank this distracting pattern for doing it's best. It's trying to keep you from ejecting something vital. As we know from Star Trek, you can't eject the core. Bad things happen.

Our core imprinting is made from our essence. Imprinted energies need to be freed rather than deleted. A core imprint is something like a watermark, etched into the luminous core that we are. We've carried it for so long that we feel like it's part of us.

Emily dreamed about the fall of Atlantis. She never told anyone, but was sure these were past-life memories. These memories were a significant influence on her. As Emily studied and learned, she became aware that what she thought of as her Atlantean karmas were those she chose to work on in this life. She knew she could use a pivotal lifetime like this one to work through and clear the patterns.

One of Emily's core imprints, the one she chose to carry, was of having failed Source by allowing Atlantis to destroy itself. This failure and atonement pattern was near and dear to her for some reason. She didn't know why. Her mind/ego had no idea that these karmas, and the atonement agenda they set up, were imprints she had chosen, nor that they could be dissolved! Her awareness knew better. At her center, she was aware that this, too, was a set of egoic misperceptions.

This lifetime is an opportunity to transform our old agendas and take on a whole new set of projects at higher frequencies. We must make a conscious choice for this to happen.

The period between 2020 and 2030 is a huge opportunity to release whatever core projects you've been working on for the last cycle, or that you came into this world to *fix*. Our old agendas need to go. If we don't release them, we become a massive, bloated caterpillar, whose leaf supply lives at lower and lower vibrations. We can't get high, meaning ascension, on that supply.

Imagine yourself moving completely into Divine expression, without having to know what that is. Choose not to get stuck in figuring out your Divine expression. You are a walking, breathing, *miraculous* embodiment, a particle in the Divine wave. And you are in a body to learn and to play. Remember that, as you move your distractions and core imprinting through the cocoon phase, into your chrysalis of transformation, and let yourself fly home.

What Will You Make REAL?

New world. New realities. Clean slate. Fresh start. What does it mean, if your intentions and choices are not focused, creative, and therefore empowered?

As you learn to be held, and to feel Her flow more and more, the function of owning your choices becomes more and more powerful.

Intend. Decide. Commit to the follow-thru.

When you aim for a vision without doubt or deviation, according to Universal Law that vision must manifest. It will do so because you have made it *matter.* I'll reiterate, what matters, manifests.

Without the moment to moment *presence* of follow-thru, your intentions will not be realized. Without a conscious decision to make something so, intentions and follow-thru lie fallow.

Rather than focus on what is left to clear or any other ongoing self-improvement project, it is hopefully clear to you by now that you must let your mind and body rest in the certain knowledge that your intentions are bearing fruit. Focus on the essence of your desired manifestation and let Her manage how the details come together through you.

So, what do you want to make real? What are your intentions for the on-going adventure of sand painting after sand painting, starburst after starburst, your role in the Infinite flow of creation? What will your contribution be?

What would you like to see unfold? Imagine yourself as a flower. What opens from the bud?

Imagine yourself as a work of art. How does it come into form? How does it change?

What matters manifests

How do we learn to know what truly matters to us and what to manifest in our lives?

First, look at what is currently manifesting or presenting for you in your life. Observe the situation, circumstance, person, place, or thing through the lens of knowing. This situation is manifesting because something about it matters to you. We all manifest the experiences of our lives, all the time. Manifestation occurs through resonance. We can resonate "for" something, meaning we like or prefer it, or we can resonate "against" something, meaning we dislike or wish to avoid it. The charge on the resonance is the same. Making resonance conscious is key. So is learning the Law of Three.

Would you like to bring manifestation into consciousness? Would you like to understand how the Law of Three, the principle of the Trinity, is the foundation for manifestation in this world? Keep reading.

Principles of Manifestation

The Law of Three. In this world, it takes the vibration of three to manifest anything. Before your mind leaps to the obvious, as in "Father, Mother, Child," ask it to be still and remember what the Oneness knows.

We all live in three experiential realities, all the time. We experience through thought. We experience through feeling. We experience through emotions. A truth that the Masters know and utilize is that when thought, feeling, and emotion are brought into divine alignment, manifestation occurs.

Using the example of Michelangelo's statue of David, we may remember that he, like other illumined artists, maintained that the David was always there, within the stone. Michelangelo only "set it free" by listening intuitively to what wanted to emerge. He called the image forth from the living material of the stone. He felt what wanted to manifest. He thought about what it might look like. He experienced the passion that creativity simply is. He allowed this alignment to flow through his body from Her, the Creatrix of us all. The Source, that is the dark, comforting womb of wisdom as well as the Infinite Light. This alignment created a work of wonder from a block of stone, chosen for its singular vibration.

In order to manifest a state of being, we must align with that vibration. But first, it has to matter to us. Whatever we are choosing to create/become has to matter more than all the other distractions of our days.

You may say you want to manifest lots of things. Wonderful! The first step is to find the common thread of Oneness, the current in the Infinite Sea, that carries the frequency wave of everything you want to manifest. In other words, find the highest vibration, the feeling, of what all of your desired manifestations have in common. Give it a thought form. An idea your mind can grasp. Then, find the emotions like joy, excitement and wonder that you intuitively know you will feel when your manifestations have come to pass.

Move thought (mind), feeling (Spirit), and emotions (body) into the vibrations of becoming this wave. Now... Let go of thinking about it. Practice being this alignment. A particle within Her creative flow and the flow within Her particle. When your alignment within Source takes over, your manifestations will appear and your life will change.

Manifesting in collaboration is the same. Use the Trinity structure to envision Her field as the well from which your dream is birthed and the manifestation of its light. There is only Oneness. Her infinite grace. From this well we call forth our desires and watch Her manifest them from light. As we become this collaboration with All That Is, we learn to lean in together, in triangular, triskele, or cone form. Focus on Source, and the foundation of your manifestation will form beneath your collective feet.

We create but do not *control* our experience of reality

We do, however, have a choice as to what we choose to experience and how we relate to our experience. Another important facet of the Law of Three is in our relationship to the Trinity of Intent – Allowing – Receiving.

We intend, as described in the information above. We learn to allow, by putting the outcome squarely in Source's domain. In all of life, it is important to remember that the "how" is up to Source. She is the ultimate do-er. If we allow Her to be that, and to take care of all of the "hows," our manifestations become miraculous. Humans so often ignore the little, everyday miracles of life! Then, we become disappointed when the "big" miracles we ask for don't show up the way we want them to!

Let Her be the do-er. All hows are up to Her.

Then, we open to receive what we desire in the way She will deliver it. This may or may not be in the ways we thought were possible, or even in the way we thought we wanted things to happen. Usually not, truth be told. That is because She knows what our hearts truly desire and is able to manifest what we yearn for in ways we could not imagine. Remember, what you yearn for, yearns for you.

Being open to receiving from Her is a choice. The simplest way is to become Her wave of creative receptivity. When we embody this quality, all that we desire is already present. It only needs to be brought into physicality. We can practice this by feeling "Thank you, that this is manifesting through Grace in divine timing, how and when it is optimal."

Beyond the Butterfly

Ascension through our physical bodies means keeping what we chose as our butterfly configuration and moving beyond that into something more fluid.

Years ago, when I took Reiki initiations, my teacher told me she saw a strange configuration in my energy field. She was looking at a butterfly, but its structure looked like wire or metal. Too rigid for flight or for the freedom a butterfly represents.

Shortly before writing this book, I saw the same thing in one of my meditations. Only this time, the butterfly-like compartmentalization was present but sort of greyed-out. No more wire or hardness, but the imprint remained.

I was quite surprised. The faded imprint spoke to the dissolution I've worked with over the years, but still the impression, the configuration imprint was in place. When I asked where I was still holding this, my physical body answered, "here."

I asked, "what do I need to let go of to assist you in releasing this?"

My body answered, "yourself." I had no clue where to go from there or what to do. And, so, I asked Her.

"Even this, you must give to me, though you believe you did so long ago."

The tears that followed her voice were tears of relief and joy.

Conclusion

I hope the information in this book has been helpful to you. The practice of letting go and letting Source become the do-er, the agent of direction in your life, assists you in understanding your evolutionary process, that of the multi-verse and beyond.

We don't know what we don't know. There is always more and Infinitely so.

I hope you will join Her journey as Infinite Oneness, in a more conscious way.

About the Author

Nalini is an internationally known author, blogger, spiritual teacher and transformational seer. She has been writing and teaching for nearly 30 years, advising those who choose to live a Source-directed life and further the development of expanded consciousness in practical ways.

Nalini is the author of several books, including Walk A(New)Way, and her latest, Becoming Oneness. She is not affiliated with any group, organization or religion.

From the author:

"Writing is something I have always done. As a child, I immersed myself in stories of nature, and of the heart. Always a voracious reader, I learned the craft of writing by observation. What turns of phrase best express the essence of each moment, scene, or feeling? Some of my greatest teachers have been the well-crafted books I've read.

'The hands are connected to the heart,' ~ anon. The path of the Author chose me by way of the heart. When love moves through me, I want to write about it, to capture the essence and wonder of experience in the written word. There are books in my library that I read again and again, gleaning new wisdom from them with each perusal. I aspire to the creation of resources like these.

As a life-long intuitive, clairvoyant, clairaudient and clairsentient perceiver, the Divine sees through me into the sacred architecture of alignment. I have spent this lifetime studying vibration, perception, and consciousness. Each path I have walked, in this and other lives, has brought a gift of understanding. In my journey into the depths of the Great Mother, the Source of us all, I found Home. I am THAT. And I am grateful."

Bibliography

Links

Suri, Sana, Aug 1 2014, Despite metamorphosis, *moths hold on to memories from their days as a caterpillar*, theconversation.com, June, 2020:
https://theconversation.com/despite-metamorphosis-moths-hold-on-to-memories-from-their-days-as-a-caterpillar-29859

Hiskey, Daven, Oct 28 2011, *Caterpillars "Melt" Almost Completely Before Growing Into Butterflies in the Chrysalis*, todayifoundout.com, June 2020:
http://www.todayifoundout.com/index.php/2011/10/caterpillars-melt-almost-completely-before-growing-into-butterflies-in-the-chrysalis/

Books {Kindle Editions}

Lipton, Dr. Bruce H. Oct. 13th, 2015, *10th Anniversary Edition The Biology of Belief*, Penguin, Random House

Lipton, Dr. Bruce H., Baerman, Steve, Sept. 15th, 2009, *Spontaneous Evolution*, Penguin Random House

Myss, Carolyn, Sept. 4, 2013, *Sacred Contracts*, Random House LLC

Paulus, Trina, July 14th, 2017, *Hope for the Flowers*, Amazon Services, LLC

Printed in Great Britain
by Amazon